From School to Landing Craft

A Young Man's War In Letters

– C.M. WILES –

An environmentally friendly book printed and bound in England by
www.printondemand-worldwide.com

Mixed Sources
Product group from well-managed forests, and other controlled sources
www.fsc.org Cert no. TT-COC-002641
© 1996 Forest Stewardship Council
FSC

PEFC Certified
This product is from sustainably managed forests and controlled sources
www.pefc.org
PEFC
PEFC/16-33-415

This book is made entirely of chain-of-custody materials

FastPrint Publishing
www.fast-print.net/store.php

From School to Landing Craft

ISBN 978-178035-021-9

First published 2011 by
FASTPRINT PUBLISHING
Peterborough, England.

For my father and mother

Contents

List of Figures

Introduction

Like many of his generation who went to war my father, Richard Charles Wiles (RCW), said little about his active service experiences. Whether he discussed the day to day events of the conflict with his parents or with friends who had shared similar experiences is unclear but evidently periods of leave were spent less in morbid reflection than a social round of frivolity and relaxation. After the war there was a new life to be grappled with. So neither of his sons had much idea about the details of the eight years from leaving school (1939) to leaving the navy and getting married with a civilian job (1947). We knew of active service in the Royal Navy Volunteer Reserve (RNVR), of a decoration, of cold and seasickness, we heard odd remarks vouchsafed for instance after a film about the war. Did we ever ask him about those times? Probably we did not: perhaps we subconsciously adopted avoidance of the issue because of age, deference or 'best left'. His naval uniform (rank of Lieutenant) hung in a cupboard in his parent's house in the 1950s, a choice item for children to dress up in. However the connection between the clothes and the experiences of the person who properly wore them was never made by us. Our mother, whom he met in Brugge (Bruges) in 1944 (following admission to hospital after injury during the actions for Antwerp) and married in 1947, later hinted at appalling incidents which he had related, and of nightmares experienced years after, thus indicating the profound impact events had had on him. Such nightmares were a feature of his delirium during his terminal illness prior to his death at the age of 72.

Eventually, following the deaths of RCW and his parents, a series of letters between him, his parents, brother and friends came to light which covered the period from his last year at school in 1939 to the end of the war. I am uncertain how many are missing in the sequence but some certainly are: sometimes a feeling is created that one would love to have known the reply to a particular letter. Letters, even if not censored, probably only carried information which it was felt necessary to communicate during absence: much verbal communication about events, not alluded to in the letters, must have occurred during periods of leave. Naval censorship was quite restrictive and little information emerges to give form and substance to the real experiences he was having when the letters were sent. The major information often lies in the address shown on the envelope, the letter heading address (if any) and the presence of a censor's stamp. Letters from RCW to home were often mundane, with requests for various items, information about travel, expectations about leave and the like. Those from his parents to him, in part prosaic, were nevertheless often informative about the War, its effects on life at home in suburban Surrey and at his father's work in London. Additionally his father's letters contain strong hints of parental anxiety relating not only to the war itself but the 'moral traps' which the war brought in its wake. The juxtaposition of the tragic with the trivial is a frequent feature. Together these letters cast light on the life of a young man brought up in a comfortable suburban home and at public school and then, aged 19, thrust unexpectedly into a major conflict. The plan of this book is simple: to give an outline of RCW's war based mainly on official documents and to follow this with an edited series of quotations from the letters which essentially "speak for themselves". Extraneous narrative is minimal.

It has been necessary to ascertain the 'facts' of what RCW was doing from clues in the letters and a certain amount of guesswork. The acquisition of his full service record and the availability of records in the National Archives at Kew has helped greatly. Even with those documents, however, it has been difficult to get 'inside' the action and understand the details of his personal involvement, let alone 'what it was really like' or how that may have affected him. I have, first, set out a short biography of RCW, then the facts of his naval record including some detail about the award of his Distinguished Service Cross - a source of great pride to both him and his family. This is followed by a series of extracts taken from letters, chronologically arranged and selected for content which broadly pertains directly or indirectly to the war. I have provided some explanatory material in footnotes and appendices to flesh out aspects of certain places, events and actions of interest.

The letter writers, other than close family or those in the public domain, have been anonymised; the names of most individuals referred to within the letters have been edited to a reference initial(s).

Sources of information are acknowledged in footnotes but I cannot personally vouch for the historical accuracy of all. I am grateful for the assistance which several organisations, website owners and archivists knowledgeable about the Royal Navy Volunteer Reserve (RNVR) and Landing Craft gave me, in particular Tony Chapman, Official Archivist/Historian, LST and Landing Craft Association (Royal Navy), Geoff Slee of the Combined Operations website, Dave Hills of the South West Maritime History Society, and JN Houterman Inquiry RNVR Officer at http://www.unithistories.com/officers/RNVR_officersW.html, who provided invaluable ideas and prompts. For six postcards herein, which belonged to my father, I have not, despite a search in good faith, been able to establish if there is still an existing copyright.

I am most grateful for the many family photos, helpful comments and information given to me by John Wiles (my father's brother, author of several of the letters and also in the RNVR during the war). I am very appreciative of the help, ideas, useful websites and comments given by David Wiles (RCW's son & my brother) and also of the invaluable critical editorial advice, suggestions and constant encouragement given to me by Jancis my wife.

Mark Wiles
June 2011

The People

Richard ('Dick') Charles Wiles (RCW) was born on April 9th 1922 in Streatham, south London. His parents were Charles Ernest Wiles (CEW) from York then aged 44 and Ottilia Louisa Wiles (OLW) from Barnes then aged 27. His brother John Randolph Wiles (JRW) was born in 1925. RCW and JRW attended Charterhouse School in Godalming from the age of 13. CEW worked in design and advertising initially, later becoming a director of Harrods and Paquin's fashion house and working at Dorlands advertising agency. OLW worked in the personnel department at Harrods before (and after) her first marriage in 1917: her two sisters also worked there for a time. OLW's first husband Sidney Wilkins died following an inoculation only a few months after their marriage in 1917 and she married CEW in 1920: from 1939 she was intensively involved with the Women's Voluntary Service (WVS) for Beddington & Wallington: she became Centre Organiser, was awarded the MBE (1956) and made Freeman of the Borough (1962). RCW married Hélène Geldof in 1947 having met her at the end of 1944 in Brugge (Bruges) following his hospitalisation there for an injury: they had two sons Mark (born 1948, author of this account) and David (born 1952) but were divorced in 1956. RCW worked in the retail trade at DH Evans (1940-41), Dickins & Jones (1947-51), Walsh's (Sheffield) from 1951, Harrods (1956-7) and the Civil Service Stores (London) from 1957 where he became managing director retiring in 1981 following ill-health. He married Catherine Gilderdale (née Mitchell) in 1962 who died in 1985. RCW died in 1994 aged 72 years.

The account below is a summary of service and wartime experience based on RCW's service record, letters between RCW and his family and friends, and annotated photographs. Other material from the National Archives or internet sources is referenced in footnotes.

Fig 1 RCW as Ordinary Seaman Oct 1941

Fig 2 RCW appointed acting temporary S/Lieut Nov 1942

Summary of Naval Service

The following pages list the chronology of RCW's naval service as far as I can ascertain it. Much of the data was obtained from his service record. However, although the service record often lists a shore base attachment, it gives little or no systematic information about active service duties. For these I have had to rely on some reports in the service record, his letters, a few photographs that he annotated and his DSC recommendation. Those unfamiliar with naval records need to be aware that the designation 'HMS' does not necessarily indicate a British ship which floats! It often refers to a shore base. Many of the shore bases are so-called 'Combined Operations' establishments around the UK. 'Combined Operations' is explained more fully below and the bases shown on a map (fig 4). Unless otherwise indicated all placements have been confirmed from RCW's original Certificate of Service (as a rating) and from a copy of his Service Record (as an officer). As well as listing the attachments I have included some brief notes, illustrations or other details where appropriate and available. More personal detail about time spent at the various establishments emerges from Section 5 – letters between RCW and family and friends.

Sept 3rd 1939	Outbreak of World War II
Oct 23rd 1941 to Dec 11th 1941	HMS *Royal Arthur* [1]: Ordinary Seaman (P/JX 309483) [2]
Dec 12th 1941 to Jan 22nd 1942	HMS *Ganges* - Mess 33 [3]
Jan 23rd 1942 to Feb 16th 1942	HMS *Victory* [4]
Feb 17th 1942 to Aug 14th 1942	Victory III [5] (HMS *Charlestown*, Mess 4)

Fig 3. HMS Charlestown (photograph belonging to RCW also National Archives ref 80-CF-2152-15) was a destroyer (originally USS Abbot) transferred to UK in Sept 1940. She undertook mine laying and escort duties in the NW approaches around Scotland. Decommissioned 1945 [6 7]

[1] HMS Royal Arthur was a shore based naval training establishment at Butlins, Skegness, Lincolnshire

[2] Certificate of Service

[3] Certificate of Service & RCW Letters, training establishment Shotley, Suffolk

[4] Certificate of Service & RCW Letters Mess 3G, Royal Naval Barracks, Portsmouth

[5] Certificate of Service

[6] http://en.wikipedia.org/wiki/USS_Abbot_(DD-184) (http://creativecommons.org/licenses/by-sa/3.0/)

[7] http://www.naval-history.net/xGM-Chrono-11US-Charlestown.htm

Aug 15th 1942 to Nov 19th 1942 HMS *King Alfred* [8]

RCW undertook his officer training at HMS King Alfred in Hove, Sussex. An extract from the reference in footnote 8 states "... In 1939... the Navy was searching for a site for a training depot for officers of the Royal Navy Volunteer Reserve (RNVR)...The Admiralty immediately requisitioned the leisure centre and on 11 September 1939 commissioned it as HMS *King Alfred* under the command of Captain John Pelly. The first trainees arrived the same day and by May 1940 1,700 men had passed through the base. Most of these were members of the pre-war Royal Navy Volunteer (Supplementary) Reserve (RNV(S)R) (The RNV(S)R had been formed in 1936 for *gentlemen who are interested in yachting or similar pursuits* and aged between 18 and 39). With the mobilisation of the members of the RNV(S)R being completed, the role of HMS *King Alfred* changed to training new officers of the RNVR... Mowden School, taken over in 1940, became known as HMS *King Alfred II* or HMS *King Alfred (M)* while Lancing College, taken over in 1941 became HMS *King Alfred III* or HMS *King Alfred (L)*. The Hove site continued to be referred to as HMS *King Alfred* or sometimes HMS *King Alfred (H)*. A training course consisted of ten weeks, the first two weeks at HMS *King Alfred II*, then six weeks at HMS *King Alfred III* and the final four weeks at Hove... the men emerged as Temporary Acting Probationary Sub-Lieutenants and attended further training at the Royal Naval College, Greenwich before being posted operationally."

A report on RCW described his character as "VG": and his Efficiency as "Superior".[9] On Oct 22nd 1942 he received an "Outfit gratuity" of £45.[10]

Nov 20th 1942 to Dec 12th 1942 HMS *King Alfred*

"... after completing the preliminary period of his training in H.M.S. King Alfred as a SPECIALLY SELECTED RATING has been promoted to the rank of TEMP ACTING SUB.-LIEUTENANT R.N.V.R".[11]

---

[8] http://en.wikipedia.org/wiki/HMS_King_Alfred_(shore_establishment_1939), (http://creativecommons.org/licenses/by-sa/3.0/)

[9] Certificate of the Service: RNVR Training establishment Hove, Sussex

[10] Service Record

Dec 1942 HMS *King Alfred*

"A well educated and quite pleasant young officer who did not show very good results in the Course. He has reported that he is inclined to be sea-sick but he seems to have plenty of determination and should get over this" [12]

Dec 13th 1942 to Dec 31st 1942 HMS *Quebec* Inverary, Argyll-shire.

This was one of many shore based establishments given over to so-called Combined Operations. A map (fig 4) shows the sites of these. RCW was based for varying periods at a number of different Combined Operations bases.

Report for landing craft training as Boat Officer (B.O.) "Keen, reliable, capable".[13]

The following two extracts explain the concept of 'Combined Operations":

"Churchill and his planners knew that when the invasion of Europe began the Allies would need a well trained and equipped invasion force drawing on the resources of all three services. Such was the magnitude of the task assigned to Combined Operations in terms of the numbers to be trained, the diversity of the training and the procurement of equipment that a total of 45 Combined Operations Establishments were set up in the west of Scotland and the south of England." [14]

"The Combined Operations Command was set up by Churchill in the spring of 1940. From 17/07/40 to 27/10/41 Admiral of the Fleet, Roger Keyes held the post of Director of Combined Operations. He was succeeded by Lord Louis Mountbatten who held the redefined post from 27/10/41 until he moved to Burma in October 1943. Major General Robert Laycock then held the post until 1947. Combined Operations made a huge contribution to the successful outcome of

---

[11] Original certificate of promotion

[12] Service Record

[13] Service Record

[14] Extract from: http://www.combinedops.com/Training%20EST%20UK.htm.

the Second World War by planning, equipping and training for offensive amphibious operations after the evacuation at Dunkirk in June 1940. In the ensuing years there were many raids and landings mostly against the Axis forces from Norway in the north to Madagascar in the south and from the Mediterranean in the west to the Far East, culminating in the D-Day Invasion on the beaches of Normandy on the 6th of June 1944. The Command drew on the best practices and expertise the Royal Navy, the Army and the Royal Air Force had to offer to create a unified force. Many of their top planners and experts formed the nucleus around which the Command was formed and, as the requirements of offensive operations took on an international dimension, the service personnel of many Allied countries proudly wore the Combined Operations badge." [15]

[15] Extract from: http://www.combinedops.com/index.htm

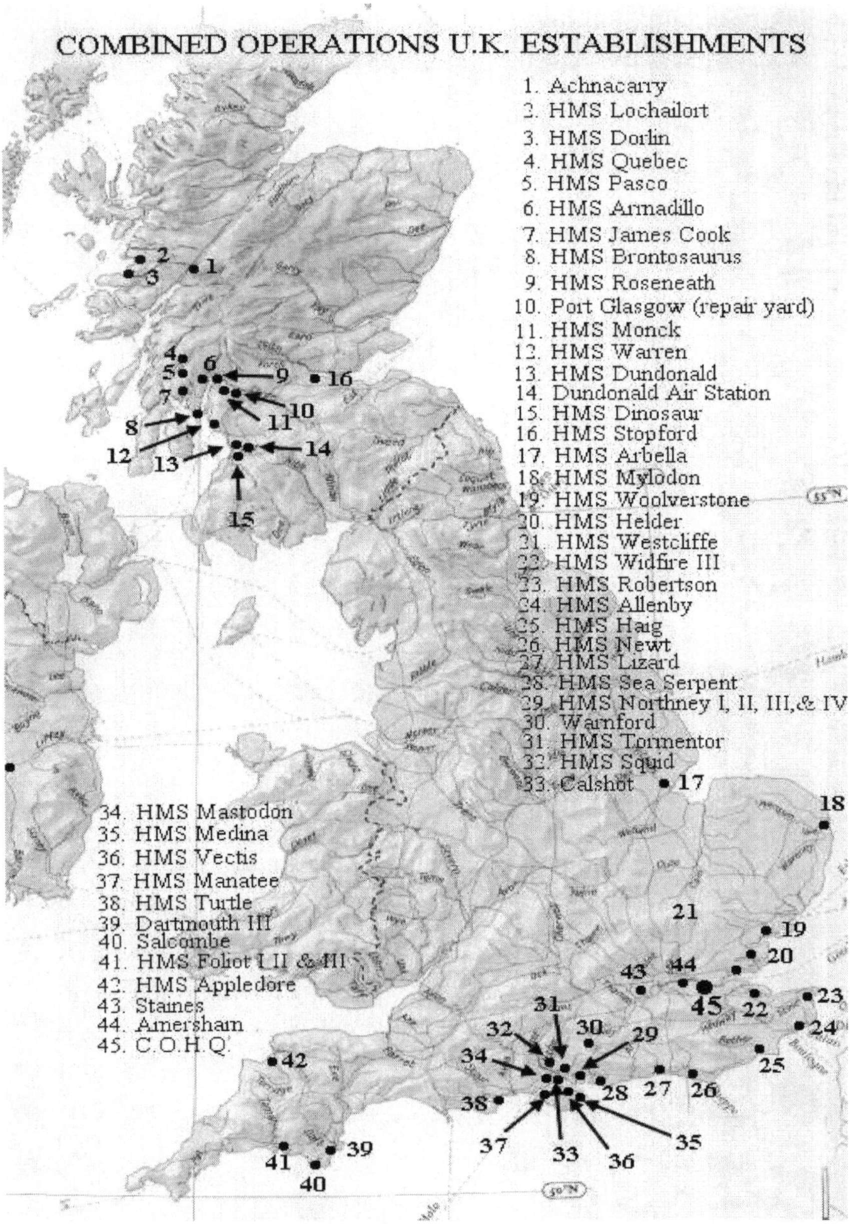
COMBINED OPERATIONS U.K. ESTABLISHMENTS
1. Achnacarry
2. HMS Lochailort
3. HMS Dorlin
4. HMS Quebec
5. HMS Pasco
6. HMS Armadillo
7. HMS James Cook
8. HMS Brontosaurus
9. HMS Roseneath
10. Port Glasgow (repair yard)
11. HMS Monck
12. HMS Warren
13. HMS Dundonald
14. Dundonald Air Station
15. HMS Dinosaur
16. HMS Stopford
17. HMS Arbella
18. HMS Mylodon
19. HMS Woolverstone
20. HMS Helder
21. HMS Westcliffe
22. HMS Widfire III
23. HMS Robertson
24. HMS Allenby
25. HMS Haig
26. HMS Newt
27. HMS Lizard
28. HMS Sea Serpent
29. HMS Northney I, II, III,& IV
30. Warnford
31. HMS Tormentor
32. HMS Squid
33. Calshot
34. HMS Mastodon
35. HMS Medina
36. HMS Vectis
37. HMS Manatee
38. HMS Turtle
39. Dartmouth III
40. Salcombe
41. HMS Foliot I II & III
42. HMS Appledore
43. Staines
44. Amersham
45. C.O.H.Q.

Fig 4: Map of Combined Operations bases (from reference in footnote 14).

Jan 1st 1943 to Jan 9th 1943 — HMS *Helder* (shore base Fig 4), Brightlingsea.

Boat Officer landing craft training for Combined Operations.

Jan 10th 1943 to Jan 31st 1943 — HMS *Quebec* (shore base Fig 4)

Boat Officer: report "Very keen and capable officer. Good power of command. Entirely satisfactory"[16]

Feb 1st 1943 to Feb 21st 1943 — 126 Flotilla, HMS *Foliot*, Plymouth (shore base Fig 4) (Boat Officer)

Feb 22nd 1943 to Feb 27th 1943 — HMS *Drake* (RN shore establishment, Devonport) (Boat Officer)

Feb 28th 1943 to Mar 5th 1943 — HMS *Foliot* (shore base Fig 4) Boat Officer

Mar 6th 1943 to April 2nd 1943 — HMS *Prins Albert*

Fig 5. HMS Prins Albert on Loch Fyne 1943 (source of photo RCW). MV Prins Albert, launched in 1937 was Belgian, gross tonnage 2938 and could reach 25 knots. She was taken over by the British Ministry of War Transport 1940 and rebuilt as an armed auxiliary transport ship. She was at Dieppe in 1942, on combined operations in Norway in 1942, Sicily/Italy in 1943, Normandy in 1944, and in India & Burma 1945.[17]

---

[16] Service Record

[17] Text information in legend based on: http://www.doverferryphotos.co.uk/pastandpresent/pa2.htm

Apr 3rd 1943 to May 8th 1943	HMS *James Cook* (shore base Fig 4)

Included 2 weeks Beach Pilotage Course[18] as Boat Officer (Report: "A keen officer with plenty of common sense – industrious but a little slow. He will improve with more experience. Always cheerful, willing & interested")

May 9th 1943 to July 14th 1943	126 flotilla Roseneath, Dumbartonshire, Scotland (see Fig 4)

Boat Officer Promoted from Temporary Acting S/Lt to Temporary S/Lt May 20th 1943.

("Tropical kit allce £10")[19]

Jul 15th 1943 to Aug 3rd 1943	HMS *Hannibal* [20] – Algiers
July 1943	RCW is evidently heading for Sicily on MV *Llangibby Castle* (126 Flotilla)[21] (see Figs 6 & 7 below)

---

[18] Service Record

[19] Service Record

[20] HMS *Hannibal* was a naval base, commissioned at Algiers in 1943 and paid off in 1945. It was recommissioned in 1945 and paid off in 1946. (http://en.wikipedia.org/wiki/HMS_Hannibal)

[21] RCW annotated photograph (see Fig 7) on board Llangibby Castle

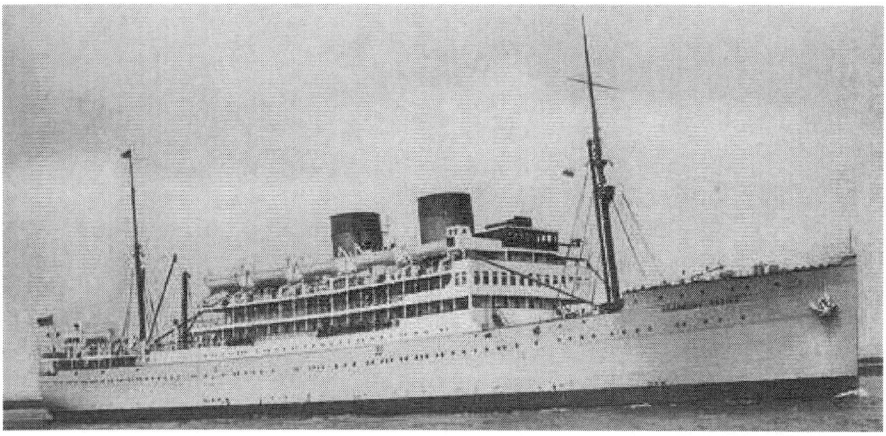

Fig 6. SS Llangibby Castle. 11951 tons, built 1929 Harland & Wolff, Glasgow for Union Castle Mail. Requisitioned as troop transport ship 1940, damaged 1940 in air raid in Liverpool. 1942 part of OperationTorch in N Africa. 1943 converted into a Landing Ship Infantry (LSI) able to carry 18 craft and 1590 troops: ferried troops in Mediterranean, then Normandy landings 1944 with 70 channel crossings. 1945 in Far East as troop transport.[22]
(Photo from postcard owned by RCW)

[22] Information based on material at:
http://www.uboat.net/allies/merchants/ships/1254.html

Fig 7 After dinner en route for Sicily July '43 on SS Llangibby Castle: RCW (left) with Lt Dormer & S/Lt Read (source RCW)

July 27th 1943	126 Flotilla HMS Hannibal, Algiers
July 1943	126 Flotilla Naval Party 869E

RCW's whereabouts are based on annotations on photographs and other material referring to the Marnix van Sint Aldegonde (see below). The Marnix took part in landings in Sicily including Operation Husky on Bark West and Sugar Beaches (see Appendix 1 about Landing Craft and some European operations).

Fig 8 Marnix van Sint Aldegonde (photo [23]) was a Dutch luxury passenger steamer built 1928: 19129 tons: reclassified as a troop transport ship for allies. Oct 1942 left Scotland for N African landings. Repaired Nov 1942 and converted to Landing Ship Infantry (Large). July 10 1943 Sicily – Operation Husky, Sept 1943 Operation Avalanche (Salerno): Nov 1943 attacked near Gibraltar by German torpedo aircraft Dornier Do 217 and sank Nov 7th 1943.[24]

Aug 4th 1943 to Oct 10th 1943	HMS *Rushorina* [25]
Oct 5th 1943	Returned from Sicily & Salerno Landings [26] [27] via Algiers in Marnix van Sint Aldegonde [28] and landed Liverpool [29]

[23] http://www.burmastar.org.uk/marnix.htm

[24] Information based on material at: http://nl.wikipedia.org/wiki/Marnix_van_St._Aldegonde_(schip)

[25] Service Record – author's note – unable to identify further details

[26] Service Record (Report by Lt Cdr Bennitt April 25th 1944)

[27] 'Salerno' ?operation Avalanche. Referred to on photo (annotated by RCW) of Marnix van Sint Aldegonde

[28] "Informal Sing" at 20.00 on 5 October 1943 – programme of singing (see fig 28)

[29] Labelled photo taken by RCW of Lt Dormer, S/Lts Alexander, Warnford, Murphy, Read & McLure on board Marnix

Fig 9 "Back from Salerno" - Sept '43 in Algiers. Marnix van Sint Aldegonde (source & annotation RCW)

Oct 11th 1943 to Oct 20th 1943 HMS *Copra* [30]

Foreign Service Leave [31] then attached to 126 Personnel Flotilla as Divisional Officer vice Warneford [32]

Oct 21st 1943 to Jan 13th 1944 HMS *Westcliff* [33]

---

[30] "HMS Copra, was never anything other than a shore base...The use of HMS Copra on grave stones, in pay books and other service records confirms that the men concerned were in the Royal Navy and assigned to Combined Operations... and that they served on and/or were lost from an unknown landing craft. I have the names of all the craft and ships assigned on D-Day and nowhere is HMS Copra recorded as a vessel." Lt Cdr B Warlow's book 'Shore Establishments of the Royal Navy' shows that parts of *HMS Copra* were located in Southend and London as well as Largs as follows; Commissioned 30/8/43 at Chelsea Court, London as Combined Operations pay and drafting office. Vacated on 3/8/44. *Copra...* to Southend by 11/43 and to Largs by 5/10/45. Copra (pay) at Largs by 3/8/44. Pensioned off 30/6/46. http://www.combinedops.com/COPRA.htm

[31] Service Record

[32] Official orders from Combined Operations HQ 18 Nov 1943

Dec 25th 1943 HMS *Ceres*

Fig 10 HMS Ceres was a C-class light cruiser of the British Royal Navy. She was the name ship of the Ceres group of the C-class of cruisers... In 1943 and 1944, HMS Ceres was used by the Royal Navy as "station ship" based at the Royal Naval College in Dartmouth. In late April 1944, HMS Ceres was refitted with radar and anti-aircraft weaponry and assigned to the US Task Force 127 to carry the Flag of the United States Navy Service Force during the invasion of Normandy.[34]

Jan 14th 1944 to Jan 21st 1944 HMS *Copra*

Jan 22nd 1944 to Mar 21st 1944 HMS *Ceres*

Mar 29th 1944 to Aug 9th 1944 HMS *Ceres*

Report on RCW "An excellent officer who for some time carried out the duties of Flotilla Officer. He is very keen, intelligent and worth a better appointment... Recommended for accelerated promotion and appointment as Flotilla Officer... Suitable to specialise in COMBINED OPERATIONS... " Lt Cdr WP Bennitt HMS Foliot (Ceres) 25th April 1944) [35]

---

[33] Landing craft base and holding base for Combined Operations personnel: Southend. Base was commissioned on 17/11/42, paid off on 21/1/46 and closed on 6/3/46.
http://www.combinedops.com/Training%20EST%20UK.htm#HMS%20Westcliffe

[34] http://en.wikipedia.org/wiki/HMS_Ceres_(D59) (photo – public domain, copyright expired)

[35] Service Record

Dec 6th 1943 to Sept 3rd 1944	Served as Divisional Officer in 552 L.C.A Flotilla
Feb 9th 1944	LCA No.552 (11-13.5t) wrecked during exercises off E Scotland [36]

June 6th 1944 Normandy: RCW was involved in landings at Utah Beach with 552 Flotilla from HMS *Empire Gauntlet.*

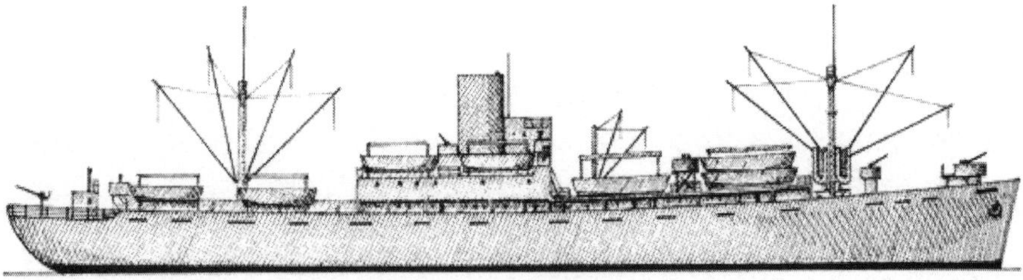

Fig 11 Empire Gauntlet was a 7,177 GRT Landing Ship, Infantry (LSI) which was built by Consolidated Steel Corporation, Wilmington, California. Laid down as Cape Comorin and completed in January 1944 as Empire Gauntlet. To Royal Navy in 1944 as HMS Sefton. [37]

A brief description of Utah Beach activities of Combined Ops follows [38]: "… A full hour before the British and Canadian landings on GOLD, SWORD and JUNO beaches the men of the US 4th Infantry Division began landing on the Uncle Red/Tare Green sectors of Utah beach. Present with them, in addition to men of the US Navy, were the Royal Navy's 'O' and 'G' LCT Squadrons, both divided across the two landing zones. Also present, delivering the initial wave of the 1st Battalion 8th Infantry of the US 4th Division, was the **Royal Navy's *Empire Gauntlet* lowering her LCAs of 552 Flotilla**." *{bold CMW} See also Appendix 1 Utah Area 1944.*

---

[36] http://www.naval-history.net/WW2BritishLossesbyName2.htm

[37] http://en.wikipedia.org/wiki/List_of_Empire_ships_(G)#Empire_Gauntlet (http://creativecommons.org/licenses/by-sa/3.0/)

[38] Extract from: http://www.combinedops.com/LCT_PAGE.htm

Fig 12a "On board 'Empire Gauntlet' 552 – Normandy Summer '44"
(source & annotation RCW)

Fig 12b "The flotilla on HMS Oceanway" [39] *but uncertain exactly where and when (source & annotation by RCW)*

[39] "HMS *Oceanway* departed Portland Harbour at 0610 hours, 6 June 1944 arriving at OMAHA BEACH at 1530 hours the same day to off-load 20 landing craft, each craft loaded with one tank. *Oceanway* sailed for Normandy as part of Follow-up Convoy B2. She departed Omaha at 2200 hours returning to Portland where she arrived at 0705 on the morning of 7 June 1944. Reassigned to the Far East in 1945. Returned to the UK in December 1946." extract from http://www.navsource.org/archives/10/12/1212.htm

Fig 13 A view from Empire Gauntlet June '44, Normandy (source & annotation RCW). Note dim reflections of officers observing sinking ship.

Aug 10th 1944 to Sept 24th 1944 HMS *Copra*

Confidential Report on RCW (Occasioned by 'Supersession of Flotilla Officer') [40]

"A very reliable officer who does not hesitate to act on his own initiative when necessary. He has held the appointment of Divisional *{Officer}* to an LC Flotilla of above average strength most ably, and should be able to perform the duties of Flotilla Officer efficiently. Slightly affected by sea sickness in small craft, otherwise very fit. Though not proficient at sports he is above average fitness. Ability to speak French – very good"

(Lt C Pratt 552 LCA Flotilla Sep 4th 1944, Capt RE Jeffreys RN Force J 'forwarded')

Also

"A good Officer who can be relied upon to carry out any job efficiently. A very good Divisional Officer, with whom it has been a pleasure to work."

---

[40] Service Record and Original note by C Pratt 4th Sept 1944

Sept 25th 1944 to Nov 24th 1944 HMS *Cricket*

HMS *Cricket*[41] was "the name given to a Royal Navy shore establishment on the River Hamble from 1943 to 1946... HMS *Cricket* was commissioned on 15 July 1943. Initially it was a "Royal Marine Landing Craft Crew Training Base". It was established as an independent command with accounts being handled by HMS *Shrapnel*. The base was later used to assemble troops and landing craft in the build-up to D-day. From 23 May 1944, during the final preparations for D-Day, the base was completely sealed... It was decided to close HMS *Cricket* after the end of the Second World War, a decision taken on 1 March 1946. The last arrivals were on 20 May 1946 and *Cricket* was probably decommissioned on 15 July 1946, three years after commissioning. Its many buildings were subsequently used for temporary post-war accommodation for the civilian population of Southampton"

Nov 25th 1944 to Dec 8th 1944 HMS *Copra*

Dec 9th 1944 to May 19th 1945 HMS *Cricket*

RCW was based at HMS *Cricket* over the period of the Battle of the Scheldt (Oct-Nov 1944) in northern Belgium & southern Holland. This was a series of operations to clear both banks of the Scheldt estuary *{see Appendix 2 for map}*, which were controlled by the Germans, in order to open the port of Antwerp to Allied shipping thus easing supply lines following the failure of Operation Market Garden.[42] The

---

[41] http://en.wikipedia.org/wiki/HMS_Cricket (http://creativecommons.org/licenses/by-nc/3.0/)

[42] Operation Market Garden (17–25 September 1944) was an Allied military operation, fought in the Netherlands and Germany in the Second World War. It was the largest airborne operation up to that time. The operation plan's strategic context required the seizure of bridges across the Maas (Meuse River) and two arms of the Rhine (the Waal and the Lower Rhine) as well as several smaller canals and tributaries. Crossing the Lower Rhine would allow the Allies to outflank the Siegfried Line and encircle the Ruhr, Germany's industrial heartland. It made large-scale use of airborne forces, whose tactical objectives were to secure a series of bridges over the main rivers of the German-occupied Netherlands and allow a rapid advance by armored units into Northern Germany. Initially, the operation was marginally successful and several bridges between Eindhoven and Nijmegen were captured. However, Gen. Horrocks XXX corps ground force's advance was delayed by the demolition of a bridge over the Wilhelmina Canal, as well as an extremely

Allies (mainly First Canadian Army) cleared the port by Nov 8th at a cost of 12873 casualties (half Canadians). Operations Switchback, Vitality and Infatuate (Capture of Walcheren Island) were undertaken.[43]

A document entitled **"Memoirs of a Landing Craft Assault Officer Lieutenant DF Brown DSC RNVR"** edited from material at the Imperial War Museum by Robert Vaughan [44] gives a graphic account of force 'H', which included RCW's LCA flotilla 552 in late 1944 - sections in italics below have been extracted from the above memoir by CMW - RCW himself is listed in the edited document on p 52 – for map of area see Appendix 2 below:

[p15]"We all now settled in at HMS Cricket...on 26th September...a force called 'H' LCA Squadron, consisting of six flotillas each of twelve LCAs now took shape. The flotilla numbers within this new force were now 506... , 508... , 509... , 510... , 550... , 552 (Lieut RE Dobson [45])... ".

[p18]"On the 17th of October three flotillas 509, 550 and 552 had sudden orders to move. They were on their way to Holland. Lieutenant-Commander S.J. Vernon, RNVR, had been appointed Squadron Officer 'H' LCA, and he accompanied these three flotillas."

---

overstretched supply line, at Son, delaying the capture of the main road bridge over the Meuse until 20 September. At Arnhem, the British 1st Airborne Division encountered far stronger resistance than anticipated. In the ensuing battle, only a small force managed to hold one end of the Arnhem road bridge and after the ground forces failed to relieve them, they were overrun on 21 September. The rest of the division, trapped in a small pocket west of the bridge, had to be evacuated on 25 September. The Allies had failed to cross the Rhine in sufficient force and the river remained a barrier to their advance until the offensives at Remagen, Oppenheim, Rees and Wesel in March 1945. The failure of Market Garden ended Allied expectations of finishing the war in 1944. Extract from http://en.wikipedia.org/wiki/Operation_Market_Garden (http://creativecommons.org/licenses/by-sa/3.0/)

[43] Extracts from: http://en.wikipedia.org/wiki/Battle_of_the_Scheldt (http://creativecommons.org/licenses/by-nc/3.0/)

[44] http://www.scribd.com/doc/6298662/Brown-Master-80814 page 15 and following South Beveland September – Nov 1944 (http://creativecommons.org/licenses/by-nc/3.0/) edited by R Vaughan as from Imperial War Museum Box Ref 92/45/1

[45] See RCW letter Oct 1st 1944 below

[p19]{?referring to all 6 flotillas} –"We remained at Ostend for a couple of days. The officers were put up at a hotel called 'Frascatis'...our stay at Ostend was just for one purpose, to have the LCAs loaded on to huge railway wagons ...one LCA per railway wagon...our train...chugged... to the dockside at Ghent... We the officers stayed at the hotel 'Chateau Rouge' overnight...We left Ghent in the morning on the 27th travelling along the canal which would take us to Temeuzen {on the West Schelde estuary –see map above in Appendix 2} in Holland {evidently 552 550 and 509 LCAs had done this route about 6 days earlier}. The other three flotillas of 'H' LCA {i.e. inc 552} meantime had already been in action. In fact they had only just completed the task of taking infantry across the Schelde and landing on the island of South Beveland behind the German forces already in retreat from advancing units of the Canadian Second Division. The opposition had been light, but they had encountered some shellfire, although suffering no losses of any sort within the flotillas..."

[p22] "There remained the problem of Walcheren. This could only be dealt with or at least expedited by assault from the sea. A large force of major landing craft, supported by gunfire from the 15" guns of the battleship HMS Warspite, and of two monitors, was to be landed from the sea on to Westkapelle. At the same time we, 'H' LCA Squadron, were to carry troops from Breskens across the Schelde for a frontal assault on the port of Flushing (Vlissingen). This overall operation was code-named 'Infatuate'."

[p23] "(at Breskens..)...an awful mess. The armies had flattened it. There was hardly a building left standing. It was also believed to be mined... Later still that afternoon we were given a briefing of sorts by Jimmy Vernon. It was bit of a risky thing to do, gathering so many men all together, because we were still under shellfire. A few ratings were in fact wounded by this shellfire... 552 flotilla arrive during the night (?Oct 30/Nov 1) - what a shambles, we were to land on Flushing at 0545. Not much in the way of briefing for them. I did not see them arrive...It seems so hard to imagine now how one could possibly have slept at all in such circumstances and knowing full well that in only a few hours time we would all be literally facing possible death and destruction."

[p25/26] "...We were en route for the 12th Canadian General Hospital in Bruges...I was shoved into a bed in the hospital...There were spare beds in my ward. They soon started to fill up, with 'H' LCA officers claiming a share...Lieutenant Dobson [46], 552 Flotilla Officer followed. 'Dobbie' appeared to have been very badly shell-shocked, although I reckon he also must have caught up with the system. He did rather better than I could though – he discharged himself the next morning and made his own way back to Breskens. ...The flotillas had been back in Temeuzen for quite some time, having first completed about a couple of days of ferrying duties. The fighting on Walcheren itself had gone on for some days but the enemy gunfire from around Flushing had been gradually eliminated (so far as the flotillas were concerned) and was eventually limited to just one battery. After one LCA had already been hit and its officer killed trying to spot this gun, Tiny Young went out and drew its fire. ... The attack on Flushing had been a success, although not without some cost. 'H' LCA Squadron had lost two officers killed and four wounded. There were casualties among the ratings but I was never able to ascertain just how many."

[p27] "The attack at Westkapelle had also succeeded but their losses had been very heavy indeed. The island of Walcheren was captured. The German garrison finally surrendered on the 8th of November. The total overall cost to our forces had been heavy. I saw it reported as over 7000 killed or wounded...29000 German prisoners were taken, and the way was now free to start clearing the Schelde of mines and thus to open the port of Antwerp."

At around this time RCW was injured:-

Oct 29th 1944	Report of a Wound or Hurt to RCW

"sustained...contusion of right ilio-costal region and lumbar vertebrae. Sub Lieut RJ Lyles RNVR who witnessed the accident considered that he *{RCW}* was then actually On His Majesty's Service in the salvaging of an Assault Landing Craft during Operation "Vitality" *{see below}* when one of the wooden slabs on the Jetty

[46] See RCW letter Oct 1st 1944 below

gave way and he fell injuring his back".[47] Evacuated to 12th Canadian General Hospital, St Andries, Brugge, Belgium.[48]

Nov 1944 552 flotilla was part of "H" LCA at Walcheren (where RCW recommended for award – see DSC documentation below): Operation Infatuate referred to the attack on Walcheren Island.

The following outlines some considerations Captain Pugsley who headed operation "Infatuate" may have had: [49]

"It was not the easiest of decisions. To say execute might mean signing a death warrant for an entire brigade of Commandos, their assault and Landing Craft and the Support Squadron who were to escort them in". His final injunction from (Admiral) Ramsey, (General) Simmonds, and Foulkes (gs - service and rank not known), his immediate Senior Officers, had been that he should not proceed with the operation unless he was facing opposition that was "not more than weak". At 0800 Captain Pugsley said there was certainly no evidence that there was such a state of affairs.

The Germans found, to their dismay that the large 88mm guns could not be lowered enough against the craft closing in on the beach. However the smaller guns were used and sank and damaged many craft, causing heavy casualties."

Feb 15th 1945 RCW, c/o 90th Field Company, Royal Engineers B.L.A.[50]

It is unclear exactly when this attachment commenced but 552 flotilla is referred to in the diaries of 90th Field Company[51] (see Appendix 3) and reference is made to the Power House at Nijmegen and 552 Mess (photographed by RCW – see figs 14 & 15).

---

[47] Original Certificate for Wounds and Hurts signed RJ Lyles, R Dobson & RCW & Captain of HMS Cricket

[48] See Nov 44 letters: & http://wwii.ca/forums/showthread.php?t=2285

[49] http://www.naval-history.net/WW2Memoir-Walcheren.htm (section 8)

[50] RCW letter and card addressed to him 7th Mar 1945 "Advice of Admission to Hospital" by JWR H Reid D/MX510767 R Navy to 6th British Hospital

[51] National Archives Docs WO 171.5452 RE Co'y 90

Fig 14 "552 LCA flotilla Nijmegen Powerhouse Mar '45"

Fig 15 "The Mess 552 Nijmegen Mar '45"
(both annotations and photographs by RCW)

Jan – April 1945 Captain AF Pugsley writes "In the last three months some 24 small operations have been carried out by craft of 508, 509, 550 and 552 L.C.A Flotillas. These operations were mounted to take either raiding or reconnaissance parties and between one and four craft were employed on each occasion. The majority of these operations were remarked on in my Reports No 0428/0.1 of 5th March and No 0600/OP.2 of 3rd April 1945." [52]

March 1945 552 LCA flotilla at Nijmegen – hand labelled (by RCW) photographs of 552 flotilla mess and the Nijmegen "Powerhouse"

March 1945 RCW is in action on R Waal 4 miles upstream from Nijmegen SE of Haalderen (see recommendation for award below, in Section 4 and Appendix 2)

Mar 26th 1945

Recommendation includes: *"The landing of a company of the Royal Scots Fusiliers at a point 4 miles up stream from Nijmegen on the North Bank of the river Waal. Map reference 7765 (S.E. of Haalderen)"*

"Sub Lieut Wiles was responsible for the four craft taking part in the operation and navigated them to the exact landing point with great skill although for the last ¼ mile the craft were under small arms fire. He remained on the beach for 35 minutes with his craft (L.C.A. 1042) and with the help of a seaman (A.B. Armitage) (sic)[53] assisted in evacuating seven casualties. After he had ascertained that there were no further casualties to be evacuated he left the beach which was still under sporadic fire. The craft was under fire until out of range but casualties were safely evacuated at Nijmegen" Signed RE Dobson LT RNVR Flotilla Officer. *{For full documentation see next section}*

March 27th 1945 onwards

Possibly involved in Operation Plunder which was the crossing of the Rhine at Rees, Wesel and other points. [54]

---

[52] Letter from Captain AF Pugsley RN (Office of Naval Commander Force "T" which included "H" LCA) Naval Party 1740, Antwerp to No 621/H.2 Allied Naval Commander, Expeditionary Force

[53] Armitage was awarded the DSM in the same action: see also letter below Capt Pugsley

[54] "The river crossing would be assisted by 552 Landing Craft Flotilla of the Royal Navy who provided several landing craft previously used in Plunder" http://en.wikipedia.org/wiki/Liberation_of_Arnhem#Allied_forces (http://creativecommons.org/licenses/by-nc/3.0/), see also Appendix 3

April 14-16th 1945

Possibly involved in Operation Anger - crossing of IJssel followed by liberation of Arnhem and clearing of Germans including from village of Velp (evidence for this is referred to in Appendix 3 and also photo May 18th 1945 and a letter in June 1945)

May 5th 1945 15.20 Naval Message

"FO 552 (R) Force T 1 Canadian Army Force T Arnhem CFCT COMMA H LCA Flotilla is moving to Nijmegen tomorrow Sunday (2) Force T First Canadian Army is requested to arrange for low level bridge at Arnhem to be broken" [55]

May 8th 1945 Victory in Europe (V.E.) day

May 20th 1945 to May 21st 1945 HMS *Cricket*

Confidential Report (occasioned by "Promotion to T/Lieut R.N.V.R.") [56]

"This officer has served as my Divisional Officer for the past 9 months & has always proved an energetic – conscientious worker. His administrative ability is outstanding & his judgement in all matters has been extremely fair & reliable. He has taken part in 8 operations including Sicily, Salerno, Normandy. This officer is strongly recommended for promotion to T/Lt RNVR & possesses a Minor LC Watchkeeping Cert (issued Jan 1944 by Lt Cdr Bennett RN HMS *Ceres*) (RE Dobson Lt RNVR 552 Flot May 21st 1945, "Insufficient knowledge" LC Eyres Captain RN Jun 19th 1945)

Then: HMS Oceanway (May 22nd), HMS *Cricket* (May 23rd-25th), HMS *Copra* (May 26th-Jun 14th), HMS *Cricket* (Jun 15th-16th)

June 4th 1945 HMS *Copra*: attached to 126 Personnel Flotilla as Boat Officer (B.O.) and is directed to repair on board that Ship at Bursledon, Southampton on 31st May 1945[57]

Jun 17th 1945 to Jul 3rd 1945 HMS *Lizard*

---

[55] Original message

[56] Service Record

[57] Official orders from HV Markham 4.6.45 HMS *Cricket*

Then: HMS Copra (Jul 4th-23rd), HMS *Westcliff* (Jul 24th-25th), HMS *Copra* (Jul 26th-Aug 2nd), HMS *Northney* (Aug 3rd-4th), HMS *Squid* (Aug 5th), 552 LCA Flotilla (Aug 6th-Aug 31st), 126 Flotilla Sept (1st - Nov 14th), HMS *Tormentor* (Nov 15th-Dec 20th), HMS *Copra* (Dec 21st-27th), HMS *Tormentor* (Dec 28th 1945-Jan 28th 1946), HMS *Copra* (Jan 29th - Mar 4th), HMS *Tormentor* Mar 5th-29th 1946), HMS *Copra* (Mar 31st-Jun 16th 1946)

August 2nd 1945 HMS *Copra*

Attached to 552 L.C.A. Flotilla as B.O. at Dover[58]

Mar 24th 1945 Member of a Board of Enquiry in HMS *Tormentor* "to enquire into the loss of one Registered package on the 25th February 1946" for which Captain AB MacBrayne expressed his "appreciation at the efficient and thorough way in which it was carried out" (letter March 30th 1946)

Sept 25th 1945 to March 31st 1946 HMS *Tormentor* (landing craft operational base on Hamble (Warsash), Southampton) Divisional Officer "... during which he has conducted himself to my entire satisfaction. A zealous and conscientious officer who should do well. A pleasing personality."

Signed A B MacBrayne Captain HMS *Tormentor* [59]

---

[58] Official orders from HV Markham 25.7.45 HMS *Westcliff*

[59] Original letter from Captain MacBrayne plus personal note sent to Home 31 Mar 1946

Fig 16 HMS Tormentor – landing craft operational base, 1946 RCW second row up 5th from left

Confidential Report (occasioned by 'Transfer to the Royal Navy' / 'Reappointment')

"A most conscientious and reliable officer who is courteous and sensible in his dealings with others and painstaking as regards the welfare of his men. A popular member of the Wardroom Mess. Keeps very fit and plays tennis, football and cricket. Strongly recommended for transfer to the Royal Navy and for accelerated promotion" AB MacBrayne Commander, RN Jan 1st & March 31st 1946

April 2nd 1946	HMS *Copra*: attached to Roseneath in pool [60]
June 17th 46 to Mar 18th 1947	HMS *President* [61]

HMS *President* was a stone frigate, or shore establishment of the Royal Naval Reserve; on the northern bank of the River Thames near Tower Bridge in the London Borough of Tower Hamlets.

July 9th 1946	War Gratuity (a payment in recognition of war service) paid (£92-16-6) [62]

[60] Official orders from HV Markham HMS *Tormentor*

[61] http://en.wikipedia.org/wiki/HMS_President_(shore_establishment) (http://creativecommons.org/licenses/by-nc/3.0/)

Mar 18th 1947 "released in Class A on Mar 18th 1947" [63]

Class A release consisted of individuals released from the forces in priority of age and length of war service, under the plan for re-allocation of manpower during the interim period between VE & VJ day (Class B was for release to transfer into industry for urgent reconstruction work).

Nov 1st 1949 Prize Money paid (£13-13) [64].

"In the 16th and 17th centuries, captured ships were legally Crown property. In order to reward and encourage sailors' zeal at no cost to the Crown, it became customary to pass on all or part of a captured ship's value to the capturing captain for distribution to his crew...The distribution of prize money to the crews of the ships involved persisted until 1918. Then the Naval Prize Act changed the system to one where the prize money was paid into a common fund from which a payment was made to all naval personnel whether or not they were involved in the action. In 1945, this was further modified to allow for the distribution to be made to RAF personnel who had been involved in the capture of enemy ships." (extract from reference in footnote 64)

---

[62] Service Record
[63] Service Record
[64] Service Record also http://en.wikipedia.org/wiki/Prize_money (http://creativecommons.org/licenses/by-nc/3.0/)

Distinguished Service Cross & Campaign Medals

This section details the documentation relating to RCW's DSC and its recommendation in March 1945. He had previously been recommended for a decoration or mention in despatches in Nov 1944.

"... It is further confirmed that, after a period of Landing Craft training, this officer *{RCW}* served with the 126 L.C. Flotilla for a brief period in 1943 and then with the 552 L.C. Flotilla from November 1943 to May 1945. He was awarded the DSC in 1945 for gallantry, daring and marked devotion to duty" [65]

Recommendation for Decoration or Mention in Despatches (transcribed by CMW from photocopies obtained from documents [66] in National Archives, Kew: italics = hand written, underlining as per original – for copies of originals see appendix 4)

- Ship etc *552 L.C.A Flotilla*
- Date *26th March 1945*
- Rank or Rating *T. Sub Lieut RNVR*
- Whether already recommended (state date and by whom)

[65] Naval Secretary letter (D/NAVSEC 12/9/7) Ministry of Defence 16 October 1990

[66] National Archives: ADM 1/30302 H&A 462

YES 14 Mar 1945: Flotilla officer {552 L.C.A. Flotilla}

- Whether previously recommended (if so give particulars)

  YES By 'H' L.C.A in November {1944} (Walcheren)[67]

- Whether now recommended for Award of Decoration or Mention in Despatches

  Decoration

- Whether recommendation is for Immediate, Operational, or Periodic Award

  Immediate

- Capacity in which employed

  Divisional Officer

- Brief Description of Action of Operation

  The landing of a company of the Royal Scots Fusiliers at a point 4 miles up stream from Nijmegen on the North Bank of the river Waal. Map reference 7765 (S.E. of Haalderen)

- Specific Act of Service for which Officer or man is recommended

  Sub Lieut Wiles was responsible for the four craft taking part in the operation and navigated them to the exact landing point with great skill although for the last ¼ mile the craft were under small arms fire. He remained on the beach for 35 minutes with his craft (L.C.A. 1042) and with the help of a seaman (A.B. Armitage) (sic)[68] *assisted in evacuating seven casualties. After he had ascertained that there were no further casualties to be evacuated he left the beach which was still under sporadic fire. The craft was under fire until out of range but casualties were safely evacuated at Nijmegen.*

Signed RE Dobson LT RNVR Flotilla Officer.

- Remarks of intermediate authority

---

[67] Recommendation for Decoration or Mention in Despatches 26 March 1945

[68] Armitage was awarded the DSM in the same action: see also letter below Capt Pugsley

Strongly recommended

Signed SJ N... Lt Commander R.N. Squadron Commander.

- Remarks and signature of Administrative Authority

This operation was remarked upon in para. 32 of Report No 0600/OP.2 of 3rd April, and was carried out in the most able and courageous manner by 4 L.C.A under the immediate command of Sub-Lt Wiles, who is strongly recommended for an award.

Signed AF Pugsley Captain, Royal Navy (Office of Naval Commander, Force "T" 4th April 1945)

- Remarks of Commander in Chief *Concur for Operational award*

- Signed Wm Burrough, Admiral, Allied Naval Commander in Chief, Expeditionary Force

April 6th 1945

Letter from Captain AF Pugsley RN (Office of Naval Commander Force "T") Naval Party 1740, Antwerp to No 621/H.2 Allied Naval Commander, Expeditionary Force [69]

"RECOMMENDATIONS FOR AWARDS

1. In the last three months some 24 small operations have been carried out by craft of 508, 509, 550 and 552 L.C.A Flotillas.

2. These operations were mounted to take either raiding or reconnaissance parties and between one and four craft were employed on each occasion. The majority of these operations were remarked on in my Reports No 0428/0.1 of 5th March and No 0600/OP.2 of 3rd April 1945.

3. In spite of low visibility, navigational difficulties, freezing conditions and enemy opposition (when surprise had been lost), on two occasions only did the craft fail to land their troops. One of these

[69] Copy of letter received by Allied Naval Commander Expeditionary Force 10 Apr 1945 from Captain AF Pugsley

was due to a dense fog and the other owing to the craft running aground on the flooded summer dyke on the WAAL.

4. The keenness, cheerfulness and devotion to duty shown by all Officers and Men has been most praiseworthy throughout.

5. Recommendations for Awards or Mentions in Despatches for the undermentioned Officers and Men are submitted for favourable consideration.

6. Order of Merit:-

OFFICERS.

Ty. Sub-Lieutenant R.O.S. Salmon, R.N.V.R

Ty. Sub-Lieutenant R.C. Wiles, R.N.V.R

Ty. Sub-Lieutenant N.R. Lee, R.N.V.R

Ty. Sub-Lieutenant M.A. Jones, R.N.V.R

RATINGS

S. Moxon, Acting Leading Seaman

D. Armitage, Able Seaman

Clifford W. Lilley, Acting Leading Seaman

Edward Glasper, Acting Leading Seaman

Alfred J. Dormer, Acting Leading Seaman

Leonard A. King, Acting Leading Seaman

John W Allum, Acting Leading Seaman

Joseph Sherburn, Acting Leading Seaman

Andrew A Allan, Acting Leading Seaman

John Kirkwood, Able Seaman

William F. Diffell, Able Seaman

Signed A.F. Pugsley, Captain, Royal Navy

Fig 17 RCW's medals in order from left to right: Distinguished Service Cross, 1939-1945 Star, The Atlantic Star with France & Germany clasp, The Italy Star, The War Medal 1939-1945. RCW sold his medals in 1990: the photo is of a facsimile and replacement set.

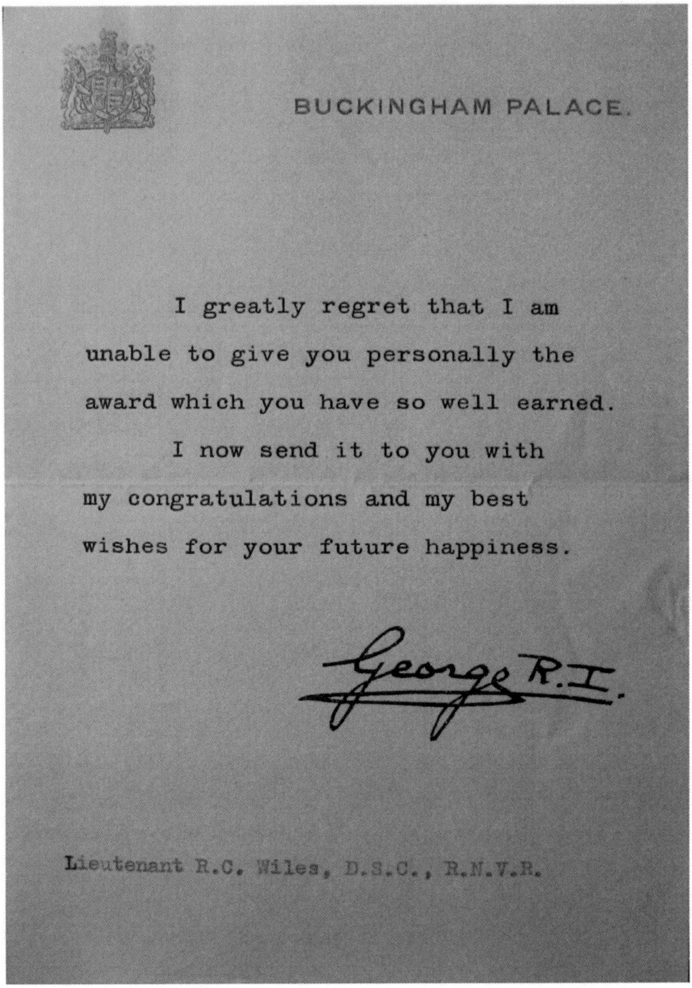

BUCKINGHAM PALACE.

I greatly regret that I am unable to give you personally the award which you have so well earned.

I now send it to you with my congratulations and my best wishes for your future happiness.

George R.I.

Lieutenant R.C. Wiles, D.S.C., R.N.V.R.

Fig 18 Letter from King George VI re Distinguished Service Cross

Decorations and mentions in despatches were published regularly in the London Gazette:

Numb. 37136 3187

THIRD SUPPLEMENT

TO

The London Gazette

Of FRIDAY, the 15th of JUNE, 1945

Published by Authority

Registered as a newspaper

TUESDAY, 19 JUNE, 1945

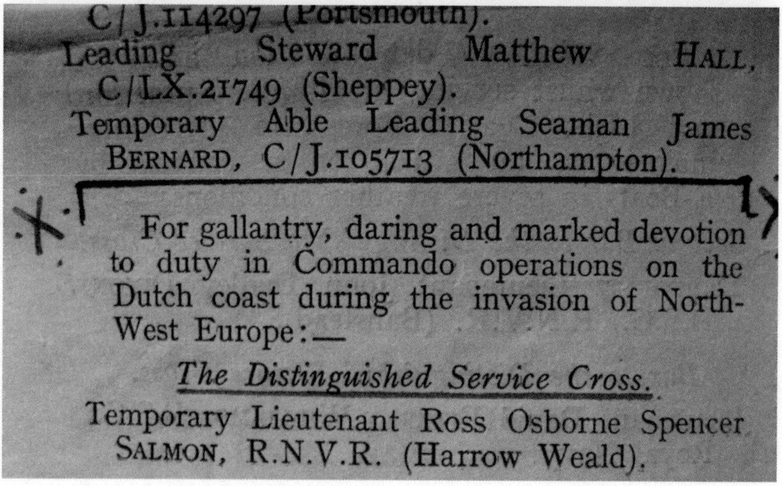

C/J.114297 (Portsmouth).

Leading Steward Matthew HALL, C/LX.21749 (Sheppey).

Temporary Able Leading Seaman James BERNARD, C/J.105713 (Northampton).

For gallantry, daring and marked devotion to duty in Commando operations on the Dutch coast during the invasion of North-West Europe:—

The Distinguished Service Cross.

Temporary Lieutenant Ross Osborne Spencer SALMON, R.N.V.R. (Harrow Weald).

ONDON GAZETTE, 19 JUNE, 1945

Temporary Sub-Lieutenant Norton Ralph LEE, R.N.V.R. (Ashford).
Temporary Sub-Lieutenant Richard Charles WILES, R.N.V.R. (Wallington).

The Distinguished Service Medal.

Acting Temporary Leading Seaman Alfred James DORMER, C/JX.394749 (New Malden).
Temporary Acting Leading Seaman Edward GLASPER, P/JX.382339 (Sunderland).
Acting Temporary Leading Seaman Leonard Albert KING, C/JX.379424.
Acting Temporary Leading Seaman Clifford William LILLEY, C/JX.379433 (Nr. Kettering).
Temporary Acting Leading Seaman Stanley Richard MOXOM, P/JX.385694 (Milwall).
Acting Temporary Leading Stoker John Wallace ALLUM, C/KX.146108 (Dagenham).
Able Seaman Douglas ARMITAGE, C/JX.372522 (New Mill, Huddersfield).
Stoker First Class Joseph SHERBURNE, D/KX.179277 (Accrington, Lancs.).

Fig 19 Citation from London Gazette (underlining by RCW)

THE LETTERS from July 1939 to 1947

{ } with italics = inserted comment by CMW: ...text omitted...

CEW – father, OLW-mother, JRW-brother. 'Home' refers to 'White House', 9 Holmwood Gardens, Wallington, Surrey throughout. Other names are anonymised.

Extracts from the letters have been commenced from July 1939 i.e. when war was clearly imminent and continued up to the time of 1947 when RCW returned to civilian life and also married. CEW was involved in work at Harrods and other stores in the group, and the advertising agencies Dorlands and Paquins - these names recur in the text.

Fig 20a The main letter-writers: (left) John Wiles brother JRW (age 20), Charles Ernest Wiles father CEW (age 67) and RCW (age 23) at White House, Wallington (home)

Fig 20b And with mother Ottilia Louisa Wiles OLW (age 50) c1945

1939

July 2nd 1939 RCW age 17, Weekites *{House}*, Charterhouse *{School}*, Godalming to CEW, Home

"... I'm afraid that my ideas for my future career were put to you in rather a sudden manner. I quite realise that I have never mentioned it before, and that any other ideas that I have told you of have been of a totally different type. Please don't think that it is a 'wild-cat' scheme as I have... thought much about it. And as I know that you have been making very great efforts to find me something suitable I hope you will understand that I of course appreciate them beyond words since I fully realise what such help can mean these days. However as you said it's no use starting up in a job one isn't keen about. To be quite truthful I don't think I'm suited to be a 'desk-man' and naturally that is why I'm considering an outdoor career. But still I of course will leave it to you as your advice will prove better..."

July 3rd1939 CEW, Home to RCW, Charterhouse

"I was rather swept off my feet yesterday... an 'old school tie' would have saved me giving myself away! Anyway there's no vast hurry about deciding and we will talk things over quietly later on. I have a perfectly open mind... my only wish is for your happiness and welfare; and while honour walks with you I shall always be proud of you. For the moment -'exams' - and all hands to the pumps!!!..."

July 5th 1939 DB (friend from home), Carshalton to RCW Charterhouse

"... all the best for your exam... Hitler and Mussolini permitting, father and I are going to France for the middle two weeks of August so I shall hope to see something of you at the beginning of the hols... "

July 15th 1939 OLW, Home to RCW & JRW, Charterhouse

"... Your favourite silk handkerchief (red!) has turned up. I have washed, ironed and put it in your drawer. Daddy took the car to Brixton this morning ... and was hauled up by a policeman for crossing on the 'red light'... a large lorry obscured them... John's sports coat is not here so presume it is at school. Have asked for his fountain pen to be sent direct... I shall think of you all the time especially of Dick <u>all next week</u> ... *"{exam week – School Cert Ox & Cam papers: a notable question in the English paper was: "Write on 'The case for or against compulsory national service'. 'for' was underlined by RCW}*

July 17th 1939 CEW, Westfield Place, Nr Battle, Sussex to RCW & JRW, Charterhouse

"... Well cheerio and the very best of good luck in the examinations – they'll soon be over – and I've no fear of the results... "

July 23rd 1939 OLW, Home to RCW & JRW, Charterhouse

"... M. *{chauffeur to the neighbours}* has been digging a dug-out all the week. Right up in the corner of the garden – near our plum tree. A massive affair with <u>steps.</u> ... thinking about you all the week. Never mind all the <u>work</u> will be worth while with Tuesday week fast approaching... will come for you outside school unless you wish otherwise... "

July 25th 1939 EAV, Cape Province, South Africa to RCW, Charterhouse

"With reference to your letter of 10th instant, I can give you the following further details of the farm advertised in the Times... " *{... evidently a citrus fruit farm in South Africa which RCW had enquired about ?purchasing... there follows a detailed account over 5 pages}*

Aug 15th 1939 RCW, Rustington, Surrey to CEW, Home

"We are having a fine time & the weather is incredible – not a cloud. Went fishing today (3 hours). Catch 1 Eel (lost), 4 crabs (put back), 3 bites!!! Well cheerio for now from Dick & John"

Aug 31st 1939 SA (school friend), Bayswater to RCW Home

"What sort of a holiday are you having? Bored yet? I am! If the crisis has not been troubling you too much and you have enough nerve to leave the shelter of your local A.R.P. *{Air Raid Precautions}* refuge what about a date? Lets make it just before the Cert results come out just in case!! Then if successful we can have another to celebrate... My future plans hang somewhat in the balance... In the event of a war I may be carted out to India with the rest of my family... my father seems very undecided at present as to what to do with my bro and self in such a case."

Sept 1st 1939 OLW, Home to RCW & JRW c/o Mrs Flowers {*Terese Flowers, married to Ted, was OLW's sister*}, Cinderford, Glos

"Daddy has just whispered in my ear 'that it is most important that you should make yourselves as useful and helpful as is possible. Having already had a little word I know you will remember won't you?... I have been the Assistant Organiser all this week at the WVS *{Women's Voluntary Service}*... We have opened, equipped and staffed 6 Canteens... When I arrived home the other day the Kitchen table was covered with apples from Dr M. *{the family doctor}* so with Aunties plums @ 16 lbs a 1/- one could have jam – plum – for the rest of ones life!!! I've really no news... dearest love and Gods Blesses Mimms. Give our love to Auntie and Uncle and say I will write in a day or two"

Sept 4th 1939 CEW, Office, Regent St *{Dorlands Advertising Agency – actually Lower Regent St}* to RCW & JRW, Cinderford, Glos

"Well, the bad business has begun, yet I expect you have heard as much about it as we have - from the wireless... most of the advertising business has simply been cancelled. The Dover Street Place *{Paquins Fashion House}* is... empty but for a porter... H's *{Harrods}* was extraordinarily empty... M *{OLW}* is at the Town Hall looking after arrangements for catering for Air Raid Wardens... Anyway she's absolutely close to a big shelter there so I am relieved of anxiety during the day time... I put some deck chairs in the cellar yesterday and fixed an electric lamp but if things don't improve I will try to get some 'reinforcement' done to the cellar... safest place in the house... otherwise we should go to the public shelter near her office in the Town Hall. The balloon barrage is now a wonderful sight - there seem to be hundreds of the balloons all over the place... As for yourselves, it was most kind of Uncle Ted to have you and still more so as things have turned out. I hope you're making yourselves useful in any way... and not causing Ted and Terese undue inconvenience... "

Sept 8th 1939 RCW, Cinderford, Glos *{Home of Terese & Ted}* to Home

"… We have made frames for all the windows here and the 'blackout' is thus complete. Don't go overdoing it at the *{Women's}* Voluntary Service, there are 20,000,000 other women in the country!!!! Also tell Daddy not to go out in the middle of the 'air raids' at any cost… "

Sept 14th 1939 CEW, Home to RCW & JRW, Cinderford, Glos

"… I 'go up' to town every day but it's a sorry business – trade… is completely at a standstill and half our people at Regent St have been put off – the other half on half pay… "

Sept 15th 1939 RCW & JRW, Cinderford, Glos to Home

"Well things have certainly come to a head. During the last 2 days about 350 kids from Birmingham have arrived and everyone us included has been busy "blacking-out" although here it's not at all necessary - I've never seen a place so black at night... Well what do you intend to do? I can't think it's anything but foolish to stay at Wallington since things are bound to be pretty hot. Did you see that Warsaw was raided 6 times in one day. But still it's up to you and I've no doubt that by now you have made some arrangements..."

Sept 16th 1939 CEW, Regents St Office to RCW & JRW Cinderford, Glos

"I was glad to be able to send Dick the wire about his success and feel sure the news will have cheered you both up no end. The details taken from the 'Times' School Supplement of Sep 15 are as follows: Pass in English Language, Credit History and Geography, Pass Latin, Credit French (passed Oral exam) Pass Elementary Mathematics, Credit Physics and Chemistry. We can discuss more about these when you return… The newspaper clerk at the station told me that three-fifths of the people must have cleared out, as they had cancelled their newspapers. He was very dejected… Piccadilly looks like a matchboard and sandbagged fortress – you would hardly recognise it. The 'tube' is closed for the duration. The busses are few. I have to walk here from Victoria and walk back – rather than join in the fight to get onto a bus… "

Sept 16th 1939 OLW, Home to RCW, Cinderford, Glos

" What suspense – then what excitement!!... Congratulations I can say no more {*School Cert results*}... Your telegram came to the W.V.S. Office... Daddy tells me he has written this morning... "

Sept 24th 1939 RCW, Charterhouse to Home

"... things here are not nearly as bad here as I expected. The 'blackout" curtains improve the place a great deal... "

Oct 1st 1939 CEW, Home to RCW & JRW, Charterhouse

"... I never even see any Air Raid Wardens now... and as for cars, well the roads just look lovely again... you'd be astonished how silent it makes the place seem... The school sent me another circular this week which points out that although 'it is impossible to say what difference it will make if a boy enrols at a Reception Unit before he is 19 it seems possible that the chance of a boy of 18 eventually securing a commission might be better if he enrolled now. If a boy of 18 wishes to enrol he must have obtained Certificate A. He will not be called anyway until he is 19 and the War Office advise that boys should remain at school until they are 19 or until they are required... We will give any boy full particulars of the method of making application to a reception unit'..."

Oct 2nd 1939 RCW, Charterhouse to CEW, Home

"... I am now taking it *{Cert A}* this term... Jameson {*Housemaster*} did not seem certain whether you intended me to leave this term or not. However as I can take Cert A this term I fail to see any further reason for staying on. As for staying till I'm 19 – well it's rather ridiculous since it means another year and a half... "

Oct 4th 1939 DB (friend from home), Royal Naval College, Dartmouth to RCW, Charterhouse

"... life down here is pretty tough but we get a lot of fun out of it. The worst thing is getting up at 6.15am. Breakfast is at 7 but we have to do ten minutes P.T. at 6.50 to give us an appetite for breakfast... (after Christmas) I come back here for another three months training. Then I shall enter the fleet proper so it looks as though I shall be able to give Hitler a kick in the pants after all... and you must really learn a few dance steps so we can go places in the Christmas leave... "

Oct 5th 1939 OLW, home to RCW & JRW, Charterhouse

"To you Dick I have posted a parcel of teacups etc... Daddy says to tell Dick – go ahead with Cert A... "

Oct 14th 1939 PO (friend from home), Wallington to RCW, Charterhouse

"Howya doin'? I hear you have a study. Do you cook kippers over a gas-jet with the sharp end of a school pen?...You might as well know that you have lent me your bike. It is now in excellent condition, very clean and the puncture which was is no more and the saddle which was not straight, is... I had better tell you that sweets will be rising in price. Toffees are already up a 1d. So gorge while you may. I advise John to store. It is true that for nearly a year I have not spent more than 2/- on confectionery. But as soon as I heard that they will soon be dearer I laid in a store, like the pig that I am. Nothing of interest has happened in the Borough except for the continual collapse of saturated sandbags at filling stations where they have not yet mastered the art of spanking them into place with boards. If anything does happen, I shall let you know. Oh! Something has occurred!! Of vital disappointment!!! George F Prior has closed down for the duration!!!! I was one of his last customers on Saturday. He had to close down during the last war. He has been an Artist's Colourman for 50 years, man and boy, in Wallington... "

Oct 15th 1939 OLW, Home to RCW & JRW, Charterhouse

"... MO *{Sister of PO above}* has got a temporary job under Carshalton Council on the Food Rationing – wages 29/6d per week to commence tomorrow. She is so excited... KO *{Sister of PO}* is waiting to be called up for the Land Army... G *{the maid}* came home in tears last night!!! It was really terrifying last evening"

Oct 18th 1939 CEW, Home to RCW & JRW, Charterhouse

"... I was glad to know you're after 'matric' before you leave –it seems pretty essential in several of the directions I have encountered lately... As for all the rumours – take no notice till you know. London's full of 'em... "

Oct 22nd 1939 OLW, Home to RCW & JRW

"... By the way Richard we have looked up 3 dictionaries and the word is ---all right---- there is no such word as alright. We were both amazed... "

Oct 29th 1939 DB *{friend from home}*, Royal Naval College, Dartmouth to RCW, Charterhouse

"You seem to have clicked nicely at Gloucester. Do you still think she's the top and are you still entertaining weekly letters with her? Bar being a peach what is she like?... The bloody war seems to be dragging on. I reckon we shall have some fireworks now America has all but repealed the Arms embargo.[70] This wretched black-out rather gets on ones nerves don't you think? ... Actually the College could be easily recognised from the air at night because the blackout system is far from perfect. There is a case of infantile paralysis *{polio}* in Dartmouth so we are not allowed to go into the town except when we are on our way to Paignton or Torquay... "

Nov 5th RCW, Charterhouse to Home

"... I've no ideas for my future yet, though I'm thinking hard!... I went to dinner with the house-master last Monday – a glorious spread starting with sherry (I didn't have any)... I'm glad to see that rationing probably won't start till after Xmas and that blackout time is to be made ½ an hour later... little else has happened. Except Cert A exam is on Tuesday! So I must away to learn up my 'Section Leading' book now... "

Nov 1st 1939 CEW, (14-16) Regent St, Waterloo Place SW1 to RCW & JRW, Charterhouse

"... I'm going to work on some stuff in connection with the publicity for 'War Savings Certificates' and it looks like being heavy going too. It's for Dorlands *{Advertising Agency}*... Going home by train at nights is an appalling business now – everything blacked-out and the carriages simply stiff with people... if Dick has any further views about

---

[70] President Roosevelt asked Congress at end of 1939 to repeal the arms embargo provisions of the neutrality law so that arms could be sold to France and Britain. In June 1940, he began providing aid in the form of Lend-Lease to Britain, which now stood alone against the Axis powers. Adapted from: http://www.nps.gov/archive/elro/glossary/world-war-2.htm

what he'd like to do… "

Nov 5th 1939 OLW, Home to RCW & JRW, Charterhouse

"… Daddy is very busy – he has been at his desk all day writing copy to 'pull at the heart strings' and make men, women and children save their pennies to help win the War. This is confidential of course as nothing has so far been publicly announced… WVS *{Women's Voluntary Service}*… They have asked me to be Centre Organiser for Wallington"

Nov 8th 1939 CEW, Regent St to RCW & JRW, Charterhouse

"…Last night… oh the job of getting home through the blackout… walking along black streets, bumping into people, getting run over – I never dreamed London looked like that after dark… Funny one of my pieces of 'copy' had the heading "Our Secret Weapon" – meaning of course our money for the Savings Certificate Ads and this morning the Committee said they thought this the best idea. When we trooped out of the Committee room the newsboy outside was holding out the 'Evening News' poster – 'Britain's Secret Weapon' – an extraordinary coincidence… All this darkness will have a sad effect on Christmas Shopping in Town… "

Nov 9th 1939 CEW, Regent St Office to RCW, Charterhouse

"You must feel as disappointed as I do, especially as this certificate *{Cert A}* seemed so important… I suppose there's no chance of having another shot at it. I only want your position to be as strong as possible when leaving time comes… I'm not looking forward particularly to tomorrows Board Meeting at H*{arrod}*s… all the best and make no mistake about the other certificate!"

Nov 11th 1939 Major Commanding Charterhouse O.T.C. to CEW

"Your boy tells me that you are very disappointed at his failure to pass Certificate A. There are however one or two extenuating circumstances: the examiners were unusually severe this year and your boy lost some valuable time at the beginning of the quarter. Nevertheless he should have passed. But whether Cert A is now very much value is doubtful. Part II (written) has been cancelled for the duration of hostilities, & so far the War Office has not informed us whether Part I by itself has any value whatever. The whole situation badly needs reviewing. If you would like your boy to have another shot in March... it could be easily arranged... "

Nov 12th 1939 RCW, Charterhouse to Home

"... I certainly felt as disappointed as you... four sections and one must pass in all... I unfortunately failed in one and wrecked everything... The whole affair has been most unfortunate since at the end of the day I was certain I had passed!..."

Nov 22nd 1939 CEW to RCW & JRW, Charterhouse

"Here I am in the 'blackout just starting my daily tramp to Victoria... I've been sweating on the National Savings stuff but so far they haven't accepted a line... everyone seems to expect the 'Nastys' to get busy here before we're much older but indeed I hope not... "

Nov 27th 1939 OLW, Home to RCW & JRW, Charterhouse

"... Just fancy Dick only 3 more weeks at school. Plug hard with the Latin & try and pull it off... "

Dec 4th 1939 RCW, Charterhouse to OLW, Home

"... Well now for those damned leaving expenses. First Tip for the Butler = 10/-, same for Butler's boy 5/- etc... "

Dec 10th 1939 OLW to RCW & JRW, Charterhouse

"... No news at all. I was honoured by an invitation to the blessing of the Ground on which the Land Army Girls are to start work in Wallington... "

Fig 21   RCW Dec 1939 on leaving school

1940

Feb 1st 1940 The Union Cold Storage Company Ltd, London EC1 to RCW, Home

"... considered your *{job}* application and regret to advise that we have decided to turn this down, the main reason for this being on account of the situation arising from the war. We wish to thank you for attending the interview"

Feb 23rd 1940 JRW, Charterhouse to RCW, Home

"... An A.T.C. *{Air Training Corps}* has been formed... these don't include me because you had to give a sort of guarantee that you will go into the air force... "

June 15th 1940 ED *{school friend}*, Bolton to RCW c/o Mrs A, ... Rustington, Surrey

"Dear Wiles... I'm hoping to get some *{holidays}* in August if we are all alive by then! Thank goodness I'm not at Weekites *{Charterhouse}*!! It must be terrible there not being allowed out at all & Exeat being cancelled. I'll bet the food is worse than ever too... I saw the flick "Gone with the Wind"... simply wonderful, the finest film I have ever seen... I have joined the Parashooters & am in the Armed Guard section. We have got 7 rifles & 150 rounds. A good means of defence against Tommy guns, I don't think? This war situation is a hell of a mess, but I just don't think about it more than I can help, it's too damn depressing... "

June 18th 1940 CEW, Home to RCW, Rustington, Surrey

"... Just a word to say I hope you are making the best of your few days' change, with perhaps just a hint that in the circumstances you shouldn't tarry too long before getting back. I leave it to you, but frankly I'm uneasy that railway conditions might suddenly become extremely difficult 'without warning' – things move at such a terrible pace these days. I attended an A.R.P. *{Air Raid Protection}* lecture in Holmwood Gardens last night... the first instruction was to 'clear the attics' – "DO IT TONIGHT" – he said. I must do something this week-end but need your help... I just can't guess at the future – nor apparently can anyone else but it's hard to find adequate grounds for cheerfulness… ”

June 19th 1940 A *{school friend}* to RCW, Rustington Surrey

“… Dear Wiles, How are you these days of bombs and Boches? London looks as though it is in an unpleasant time what with the French packing up etc. Did you join the L.D.Vs *{Local Defence Volunteers}*? Guys *{Medical School}* has quite a sizeable contingent but we are being disbanded in just under a week, as the Government says we are exempt to pass exams not fight! I was on duty only yesterday, and during the night we had our first air raid warning. I wasn’t on sentry duty at the time; but the sentries on top of our post (a 70’ foot tower) could see the anti-aircraft bursts over London. In fact I got no sleep before 5 o clock last night; still it might be worse! Or might it? I am starting my holidays on Saturday week and if we aren’t invaded before then I get until August 15th. I’m staying in Folkestone temporarily – a nice safe place of the world to be in what?… I had a very interesting few days during the Dunkirk evacuation. A lot of wounded were received at one of the local hospitals. What I don’t know about stretcher bearing now… isn’t worth knowing… there were a lot of French soldiers among them… ”

July 13th 1940 CEW, Home to JRW, Charterhouse

“… We have shut down Paquins for a month… sad business getting rid of people… whether it will ever open again is a question but I hope it will. The Paris branch is – heaven knows where – we cannot get a vestige of news about it – so how could we go on offering the ‘Paris Creations’… Dicks *{Dickins & Jones}* and the Brompton Rd *{Harrods}* sale are now finished… done about half their trade… London’s trading outlook is mighty thin. The people here seem busier than ever knocking up shelters… there’s a huge one in the middle of the road outside the office. As for home… happily nights have not been disturbed as yet… Did I tell you M’s son was drowned in the Arandora Star [71] and several of the big hotel managers in the West End

---

[71] SS *Arandora Star* was a British registered cruise ship operated by the Blue Star Line from the late 1920s through the 1930s. At the onset of World War II she was assigned as a troop transport and moving refugees. At the end of June 1940 she was assigned the task of transporting German and Italian internees along with prisoners of war to Canada. On 2 July 1940 she was sunk in controversial

(Italians). Benini the manager of the 'Hungaria' here and several of the waiters going to Canada for internment – all lost. He was a fine chap too... Several of the fellows from here are going (called up) but in a way it's perhaps as well for the business is dwindling to nothing... Of the 'war news' itself... There seems to be an idea getting round that he won't attempt to come here for a long time – perhaps a year –but what there is in that I don't know. Anyway, we're all carrying on as cheerfully as we can and I've no doubt you are doing the same... "

Aug 25th 1940 ED *{school friend}*, Bolton to RCW Home forwarded to ... Cinderford, Glos

"Dear Wiles, How are you you old stooge? Are you still working in London or have you been evacuated? ... Next month I am joining up!! I am trying to wangle a commission into the Artillery. I had a post-card from B. the other day, & he says he's joining the R.A.F. next month *{see letter Nov 12th 1941 re B.}*... How is Harrods?...I am going crazy up here with heartburn. I am absolutely crazy about a girl... but can't get anywhere, damn & curse!! We have been doing quite a bit of shooting. We got 90 brace on Aug 12th. Cartridges are getting very difficult to buy... "

Tue 1940 ?month RCW, Home to JRW, Charterhouse

"... Did you get the air raid warning last night (Mon) – we just got up for a few minutes then all went back as little seemed to be happening – apparently the town in S.W. England where the 5 people were killed was Bristol!!! – not so very safe... Thanks for the photo – I have now got a frame and mounted it... Heaven knows what's happened to her *{refers to VB... girl who had been staying with Headmistress of RCW's primary School, St Hildas, and returned to France - see later letter Feb 22nd 1945}* though – I had a letter 3 weeks ago but have heard no more since – apparently it's now quite impossible to send a letter to France... you see Rennes is in the north of France – therefore occupied by the b...y Germans. Had tea with SA *{school friend}* today – he says he's leaving for India in 18 days – that is if nothing unforeseen happens... "

---

circumstances by a German U-boat with a large loss of life. Extract from http://en.wikipedia.org/wiki/SS_Arandora_Star (http://creativecommons.org/licenses/by-nc/3.0/)

Sunday 1940 ?month RCW, Home to JRW Charterhouse

"... Nothing been happening here except I've joined the L.D.V's *{Local Defence Volunteers}* 2 evenings per week 8-10 on Tues and Fridays (There are 450 members here and not a single rifle!!!)... "

Dec 6th 1940 V *{friend}*, Cinderford, Glos to RCW, Home

" Dear Sweetheart... I am very glad to know you are still ok and still alive... We get quite a few warnings but we don't hear much. I hope we shan't do so. We've been terribly lucky... Please try to come down... "

1941

Jan 21st 1941 DB *{family friend}* HMS *Ramillies* to RCW, Home

"... Once again I will try to put my pen to paper but what I am going to say, goodness only knows. That wretched man called the censor makes things very trying. We have now got down to the regular routine of life on board and all thoughts of our leave are rapidly becoming past history. In fact now and again, we wonder how long it will be before we get our next spot. Consequently those thoughts which had first place in our minds when we returned on board are being tucked away in a corner until we step ashore again. Hence you will deduce that the flames are rapidly becoming a dull glow instead of the roaring furnace which no doubt exist perpetually in your mind. Still... letters do arrive... which certainly helps to keep the home fires burning... I recollect some way back that [we] did a lot of staff work in connection with your "affair" so we can now call it quits. Wasn't London a bloody mess after that raid on the Sunday night I was home. I can't see what military advantage Hitler hoped to attain after it but it certainly seemed to me just a case of wanton destruction. I had a rather difficult time getting over to Paddington as there were no buses at Clapham Junction. However I managed to get a taxi to Euston and from there the driver took me to Paddington... "

Feb 2nd 1941 M *{friend from home}*, Salisbury to RCW/JRW, Home

"Well I am now in the HG *{Home Guard}*. I was just issued with part of my uniform, Denims, Coat, Bandolier, belt and Boots, Cap. I am in the Mobile Column in the Lewis Gun section. Very interesting. Couldn't you get down for a week? What will you register for, RAF, army or navy?... Sorry for delay in posting *{written Feb 2nd posted 9th}*. Have since been out to demonstration & have had uniform. Planes attacked us with Gas and low level attack 20 ft, phew! Love to all M..."

Mar 9th 1941 RCW, Home to JRW, Charterhouse

"... I have just had an increase of 17/- which now means I get the enormous sum of £2 per week... Actually I have spent very little – no records or ties etc – though I go out to dinner every Thursday with B's secretary and also on Sat afternoon. Daddy knows about the dinner but thinks I go with A *{family friend}* on Sats: - still break it gently I say! She's ever so nice - in fact it's a raging inferno! Only a bit older than me - she's 28!!!!!! but there's a war on so who cares?... writing only occasionally to Cinderford, & although I had a Valentine card 1 foot square I'm afraid that for my part it's definitely cooled!!!"

April 16th 1941 DB *{family friend}* HMS *Ramillies*[72] to RCW

"... You seem to have been having a pretty hectic time of late what with that bomb in Beddington Gardens to say nothing of the secretary! I suppose the bomb must have been in Dr M's *{family doctor}* place. I'm glad to hear nobody in the White House was hurt but it seems to have done a hell of a lot of damage. Yes I did hear about the calling up of the 18s and was wondering when it was coming into effect. Still with this business in the Balkans perhaps you might go earlier. I hear the Germans are in Salonika and things seem pretty black but what I want to know is, where is our army??... Yes I do remember you mentioning something about the fair maiden... I consider it definitely bad when you admit she's rather sweet!!... Will you be glad to wear khaki, airforce blue or, the best of all, the 'senior service'?... "

April 20th 1941 (see footnote 73) RCW, Home to CEW and JRW, c/o Mrs G, Savernake, Wilts *{where JRW convalesced after peritonitis}*

"... We are both alive and well here in spite of some pretty 'heavy' nights – Friday night a land mine in Banstead Rd demolished 8 houses & damaged some 300 others. It happened at 10 o'clock – not a great explosion simply a thud – a pause, then the house shook violently thought it was coming down. Maple's in London has been burnt out[73] (last Thursday) also a large bomb in one of the turnings out of Regent St has removed any glass that was remaining in that area and very seriously damaged the brand new police station. Today the

---

[72] HMS *Ramillies*: Revenge Class Battleship 28000 tons: 8x15" guns. Around this time in N Atlantic – convoy protection – involved with German battlecruisers Gneisenau & Scharnhorst (Feb 41) & Bismarck (May 41) nr Greenland http://en.wikipedia.org/wiki/HMS_Ramillies_(07) (http://creativecommons.org/licenses/by-nc/3.0/)

[73] Maples Furniture store in Tottenham Ct Rd was burnt out in a major raid April 16/17th 1941

Home Guard had a grand turn out at 9 o' clock this morning for some general who was making a tour of the district. Anyway I was at the police station for 5 hours with 6 great lorries (hired for the occasion) which were to carry men to the various posts... just nothing happened for 5 hours – the lorry men melted away – no general came – at HQ in Wallington no one had even the remotest idea of what was meant to happen - it was lamentable. Things in Oxford St are showing no signs of improvement or anywhere in London for that matter *{RCW working at DH Evans}*... PS Hope you find the ration cards satisfactory" [John] "... M *{friend}* came up with his mother to D.Hs *{DH Evans}* last week... he's off to the R.A.F. (ground staff) tomorrow at Penarth... PS M's teeth are now practically black & his fingers quite brown (20 smokes a day average)"

June 20th 1941 RCW, Savernake Forest, Wilts to JRW, Charterhouse

"Our last night here – 7 days of wonderful weather... "

July 15th 1941 P *{school friend}*, Weekites, Charterhouse to RCW Home

"I was wondering if you would be leaving D.H. Evans soon, about the beginning of August. If you were thinking of a little toughening-up of the muscles etc before joining the Army, I know of an O.C. farmer at Ashford in Kent who wants two Carthusians next holiday..."

Sept 22nd 1941 DB *{family friend}*, HMS *Malaya* [74] to RCW, Home

"I've left the Ramillies over a week now and am in another battleship, slightly larger... We are now working up for our exam which is looming... However we ought to get a week's leave at least before going to Portsmouth... four months there... We had a very hectic day in London on the Thursday starting with lunch and carrying on into the small hours... We saw the 'Light of Heart' at the Globe Theatre which was extremely good. Then onto the Troc for dinner and dancing before a hectic taxi drive to the station... "

---

[74] 33000 ton Queen Elizabeth class battleship: 15" guns etc: at that time doing convoy protection UK to Malta & Cape Town (http://en.wikipedia.org/wiki/HMS_Malaya) (http://creativecommons.org/licenses/by-nc/3.0/)

Oct 22nd 1941 JS *{friend}* to RCW

"To my dearest with all my love for as long as you want it"

Oct 23rd 1941 RCW, HMS *Royal Arthur* Ord Sig telegram to Home

"Arrived 1.30 writing tomorrow Dick" [75]

Oct 24th 1941 RCW, HMS *Royal Arthur* to Home (as from R Wiles Ord Sig, Class S30 Division 7X, HMS *Royal Arthur*, Skegness)

"... incredibly hectic day - doctor - dentist - lectures from parson - commanding officer etc. Am in a chalet with two very decent fellows - a bed each - running water, electric light - & heaters (one needs the heat)... red roses at the front door- Getting uniform tomorrow - Could I have another pair of pyjamas please? We get up at 6.30... in bed by 10. PS One of the fellows in the hut is the chap from Wallington... "

Oct 26th 1941 OLW, Home to RCW, HMS *Royal Arthur*

"... We are both relieved to know you are so comfortable for the beginning of your training... J is coming one Saturday... guess I shall be able to entertain her for you... F has gone to Bulford Camp Salisbury Plain... Also have you answered V's letter? You had better do so... Am posting Pyjamas first thing Monday... Work hard and make good progress. It will make all the difference both during the War and after and it can be done. To us here it seems like the Boarding School days back again... MO called in this morning to say L has phoned to say she was furious M*{O}* & K*{O}* had not joined forces and would stop allowance forthwith if they did not... "

Oct 26th 1941 RCW, HMS *Royal Arthur* to JRW, Charterhouse

"... It's only 75 yards from the sea and incredibly cold & windy. I have just got my uniform and it's the very devil to put on. There's nothing on here today so am going into the town after lunch and will probably go to the 'flicks'... "

Oct 26th 1941 CEW, Home to RCW, HMS *Royal Arthur*

---

[75] RCW commences at HMS *Royal Arthur*: training establishment established near Skegness 1939-1946 (http://en.wikipedia.org/wiki/HMS_Royal_Arthur) (http://creativecommons.org/licenses/by-nc/3.0/)

"Dad's News Bulletin... Grim faced bloke calls this morning to negotiate re purchase of "Dicks Folly" *{RCW's motorbike}*... Summons for road-hogging arrived the morning you left. Lady Councillor *{OLW}* undertaking appeasement with the Beak... Mrs L. reports raid on Redcar – the few casualties cleaned up the Mayor and Corporation all in Council – all killed... RB *{CEW's boss}* said I ought to be proud of you... Don't get swelled head... Rosemary M leaves for Leeds to-day to join American Ambulance Unit (with Gertrude L)... Electric light, running water, separate beds, electric fires – make the most of them – they're costing me 10/- in £1... to be continued... "

Oct 27th 1941 JS, Grove Park SE12 to OLW, Home

"Dear Mrs Wiles... He *{RCW}* certainly seems to have struck quite a good place, all things considered... Do you think there is any chance of the WRNS *{Women's Royal Naval Service}* being so fortunate – because if so I shall seriously consider a change when I have to register on Saturday week... "

Oct 27th 1941 RCW, HMS *Royal Arthur* to home

"Yes I'll certainly take G's offer for the "Folly" *{motorbike}* there seems to be absolutely no point in keeping it... perhaps you'll let me know the amount of my fine – if any... It's incredibly cold here... so far little has happened – a trip to the gas chamber, inoculation & vaccination... photos for identity cards... went to the pictures in Skegness & had an high tea after – my appetite has grown enormously... the food is quite reasonable – only I find eating bread – butter & jam off the table with no plates rather strange!!... my uniform has to be marked... There are entertainments every evening (we knock off at 4.15) such as cinema 2nd admission, lectures, band to listen to... last Sat: the star turn being Henry Hall's pianist – who came in the same batch as myself – he was marvellous. Could you possibly send me one suit of my thick underwear and... a pillow slip. Also a pot of honey or the like... Do you know that myself and the chap I went down with were the only ones out of about 60 who didn't need teeth extracting or filling. I don't believe ½ of them had ever seen a toothbrush!!... The news doesn't look too good does it? You know I don't believe that more than 1 in every 100 ever looks at a paper & no one ever listens to the news on the wireless... "

Oct 29th 1941 JRW, Charterhouse to RCW, HMS *Royal Arthur*

"... thanks for your letter, life certainly doesn't sound too bad for you... I see you say have got heaters! Oh! Oh! What a luxury. For the last week here we have all been perishingly cold... I have just completed my quarterly grumbles and bad temper over yesterdays 'whole day manoeuvres'. We spent the time either cycling along at top speed and pouring with sweat or sitting in the bracken... freezing... while we ate our lunch... without doubt the most measly in quality and quantity I have ever experienced... The only interesting thing was a demonstration of artillery in Major Morris' words "The first demonstration of artillery given to us in the history of Charterhouse"... "

Oct ?30th 1941 RCW, HMS *Royal Arthur* to home

"... I am now quite recovered from the inoculation only felt a bit queer on Sunday but my arm was very painful & swollen... "

Nov 1st 1941 TA *(younger brother of GA, school and family friends}* to RCW, HMS *Royal Arthur*

"... I hear from S... that you get pretty short hours and so you are lucky in two ways in that you don't suffer from boredom or long hours... everything is as dull as ever: especially a certain little lady in the Staff Office. I went to my 2nd Medical and interview on Wednesday and passed o.k: mainly because the officer was an O.C. *{Old Carthusian}* also he came from Weekites... The great snag is though I am on six months deferred service. Honestly I don't know how I'm going to stick it... " *{see letter May 6th 1945}*

Nov 2nd 1941 RCW, HMS *Royal* Arthur to OLW, WVS Office

" Dear Mum... I've had 3 letters from J *{JS}* this week... Let me have the gloves as soon as possible will you – it's really dreadfully cold... P.S. Don't forget the food will you please?"

Nov 2nd 1941 OLW, Home to RCW, HMS *Royal Arthur*

"Have been wondering these last few days how you have been feeling & praying that the after effects of the inoculation etc have not proved too uncomfortable.- I know they can be *{OLW's first husband, died within a day of (in her view because of) inoculation in 1917}*... I hope you have made up your mind to enjoy the life & make some good headway. I know it's easy to talk but guess Richard Wiles can do it anyway!!... you will have received the underwear & Golden syrup. Am looking for a suitable tin to put the honey in as it would not travel in glass jars... Your case came up for hearing yesterday – have not heard anything so far. I returned the summons saying you had been called [to] HM Royal Navy... A most dreadful tragedy has befallen the R Family... On returning home Mrs R... looked in vain for T... on going upstairs she found him lying dead on his bedroom floor. He had been experimenting and died from misadventure... Coffin draped with Union Jack and Home Guards carried it. Apparently all the previous night he was on duty at the Town Hall... T would have been 18 years old today... Have commenced buying you some War Savings Stamps & will send them for your Post Office Book... Daddy & I were pleased to get your letter... they mean an awful lot to us as we shall never get accustomed to the house without you... "

Nov 4th 1941 OLW, Home to RCW, HMS *Royal Arthur*

"... Am just sending an S.O.S. to Auntie Terese *{OLW's sister}* asking her to knit some more (gloves) for you as one pair won't go far... Daddy in fact both of us are thrilled to hear you have at least been selected for the Commission Class... What does the uniform feel like? Does if feel like a sausage skin... am longing to see you in it... Yes by all means send washing home... Nothing more materialised in regard to the summons yet!!!... So pleased you went to Church... Have you written to V?"

Nov 8th 1941 RCW, HMS *Royal Arthur*, Class 161 Top Division, to Home

"... And the next 36 hours are going to be a very welcome rest after an hard week, P.T., drill, rowing, knots, semaphore etc... One night last week I walked to a little village about 3 miles away and found a W.V.S. canteen where we had the most wonderful supper for about 10d, beans on toast, 6 cheese and cress sandwiches, 4 cakes, trifle, 3 cups of tea each... It was pay day on Thursday (it's only every 2 weeks here)... "

Nov 9th 1941 CEW, Home to RCW, HMS *Royal Arthur*

"Dear Lord Admiral... Certainly the powers that be don't seem to be leaving you a lot of time to think over either your past life or your future but doubtless you still have opportunities for a little quiet and wise philosophy about things in general – which personally remains one of my few mental comforts. Please keep us posted with all developments – the items which may appear to you trivial help us largely to 'see the picture' of your interests and doings... If you 'buckle to' it looks as though you'd be safe for a commission which would be encouraging but you'll have to plan your study firmly and stick rigidly to it in the face of probably many more tempting social interruptions (which continually have a way of landing you nowhere however momentarily enjoyable they may seem). As I've said before there's only one place for a 'Wiles' though it's no use any of us expecting the road to be easy –... "

Nov 12th 1941 JRW, Charterhouse to RCW, HMS *Royal Arthur*

"... Did you hear that B *{referred to in letter of Aug 25th 1940 above}* was shot down into the sea while attacking a convoy and I don't think it is thought that there was much hope of him having got out, anyway nothing has been heard and it happened over a fortnight ago. Apparently, having dropped his bombs first, he had to keep off four Messerschmitts! We played our sole house match last Wednesday... " [see 41.29a below]

Nov 13th 1941 JS *{RCW's friend}*, Grove Park SE12 to OLW, Home

Fig 22 Postcard of "The Chalets", Butlins Holiday Camp Skegness

"... might be interested to see where the Navy of the future learns the art of tying knots!... You will see that Richard has numbered them on the back *{fig 22 is labelled 1}* & this is what he says about each one:- '(1) is exactly like the row I have to house me with the exception that those female spectres in the foreground are no longer!'... "

Nov 14th 1941 RCW, HMS *Royal Arthur* to OLW, WVS Office, Wallington

"Please excuse this vile paper but its all I can get hold of... G has sent me £14 for the bike and he will be calling for it in about 2 weeks... Re

Money: I actually get £2 per 2 weeks and don't smoke or drink but this is how it goes stamps, notepaper, toothpaste, coffee & buns in the break each morning; when I'm allowed on shore on an average 2-3 times per week always in the evening except Sat or Sun when it's 2 o'clock till 10pm. Skegness is the only place to go – 3 miles (a 7^{d} bus ride) sometimes I walk, on getting there literally nothing to do except – cinema and then a café for tea or supper. On top of that all my kit I have to have from now on – has to be paid for by me (there's supposed to be 3^{d} per day kit allowance in the £1 per week)... So doubtless you'll be able to understand there's honestly not much chance to save. The only way possible is not to go out of the camp when one's allowed which after a hard day drilling – rowing etc one doesn't feel much like doing. However I have £105 in the P.O. now & I would like to put about £95 or £100 of that in H's *{Harrods}* bank – I wonder if Daddy could get me 3% on it... rather risky if I were to have the book stolen – a very likely happening... the whole camp is having petty thefts every day... "

Nov 16th 1941 OLW, Home to RCW, HMS *Royal Arthur*

"... Will you write a similar letter to Daddy *{presumably as Nov 14th above}* as he asked me only last week how you managed on your money. Then you can ask him about putting your money in Harrods Bank... "

Nov 16th 1941 RCW, HMS *Royal Arthur* to Home

"He [John] told me that B (one of the 3 who started with me in Weekites *{Charterhouse}* is almost certain to have been killed whilst attacking a convoy (he was a pilot)... only 19... We have been kept pretty hard at it this last few days, P.T., boxing, rowing, drill – lectures etc as a matter of fact if nothing unforeseen happens I should finish my disciplinary training in the next 2 weeks and be leaving this place – for which I won't be particularly sorry as Skegness is really a land of the dead! I was in there yesterday – had a haircut & wash – cinema, tea and a walk back (3 miles) – calling in a little café on the way for toast & coffee – went with a fellow in this class who comes from Barnet... I also rang up JS... once I had moved to the head of the queue for the phonebox which took ½ hour... oh I went into a chemist to have myself weighed – 10 and ½ stone – that means about

7 lb to the good!... A parcel came from Auntie Terese *{OLW's sister}*... with an excellent pair of gloves... By the way I should very much like a 'balaclava' and a scarf, they would come in very useful for fire-watching. On Friday I had to do 2 hours from 2-4 in the morning on a tiny roof of the hospital here about 50' high. I can't say it was exactly warm... I managed to get 8 blankets [to sleep] so for that time I didn't freeze. We had... lunch... pork, roast potatoes, cauliflower, and apple pie – soup all the meals here are quite good... with the exception of breakfasts... "

Nov 23rd 1941 RCW, HMS *Royal Arthur* to Home

"... I went to Skegness for a bath last night (at the) Y.M.C.A. they're not at all bad and plenty of hot water, by the way that's not the first bath I've taken since I've been here. Since you seem to be interested in my financial state... I believe I told you before I receive 21/- per week or £2 per 2 weeks... I don't seem to be able to save more than perhaps a shilling or two as there seem to be so many little oddments which are necessities, soap, stamps, toothpaste, boot repairs, (heels just burn away here), coffee and buns every morning. Then of course when one goes into Skegness it's difficult not to return about 3/- poorer, being so cold the cinema is literally the only place to go and the fare in is 7d... Well since I started writing this, I have learnt that our class has been chosen to represent the Navy (guard of honour) at Peterborough on Thursday week – sounds good doesn't it – but all this morning nothing but drill – drill and more drill – in fact nothing else until the actual time – I expect we shall be quite worn out by then. The one good thing is though that after the show (by the way it's their 'War Weapons Week) the Mayor is going to give us the freedom of the city – everything free! I think I'll close now as it's just after lunch and there'll soon be DRILL again... "

Nov 24th 1941 OLW, Home to RCW, HMS *Royal Arthur*

"... Hope the effects of the inoculation will have passed away. It is all very unpleasant but suppose it has its good points – at least so it is said... There was a League of Nations Meeting in the Hall at the end of our road on Saturday last. The gathering got out of hand so it was disbanded. If those few people cannot agree what hope for the Nations!!!... "

Nov 26th 1941 RCW, HMS *Royal Arthur* to Home

"... It has been another hectic one so far, getting into final fettle for the Peterborough affair tomorrow – we are leaving here at 9.30 and the idea is to parade through the streets – listen to speeches – salute the mayor etc – we are being given lunch by him and tea in the Town Hall – which is one slight consolation. I've never done so much drill in my whole life before as in this last week (6 hours per day!) – we are returning about 6 p.m... "

Nov 30th 1941 OLW, Home to RCW, HMS *Royal Arthur*

"... Well you will be pleased to know that J*{S}* arrived at 11am this morning and feel sure she enjoyed her stay. We had lunch Roast Lamb, sprouts, baked potatoes, Yorkshire pudding, mint sauce and Mince Pie. We sat round a roaring fire in the lounge and had tea at 5 o clock with Daddy in the Den and listened to the Brains Trust. It was much above the understanding of us all... Daddy was top hole and J had to go in the garage and inspect the car... J looked very nice – she had a green frock with a coloured flowered necklace – very dainty. She had a nice gray coat & hat with a cerise scarf – very chic. So there you are... It's good John passing his Cert A exam is it not?... "

Dec 2nd 1941 RCW, HMS *Royal Arthur* to Home

"Just a line to let you know that I shall be home for this weekend, sometime Friday night until the 11 o'clock train at Kings Cross on Sunday night... "

Dec 2nd 1941 OLW to RCW, HMS *Royal Arthur*

"Your letter dear boy received this morning... She [JS] could come Saturday & stay but the leave is so short Daddy would like to have a little time with you I know especially as it's the first leave... Feel quite thrilled at even the prospect of seeing you... "

Dec 7th 1941 JHP *{cousin}*, Boston, Lincs to RCW, HMS *Royal Arthur*

"Dear Dick, This morning I received a letter from Aunt G *{OLW's sister}* of Cheam. She tells me you have joined up in the services and ... you are in the Navy... I shall be pleased if you have any time to spare. Could you run over to Boston – any day –... I shall be pleased to put you up... "

Dec 8th 1941 RCW, HMS *Royal Arthur* to Home

"Monday. Dear All, Arrived back here at about 3.45 and was in bed by 4. Its frightfully cold today... "

Dec 8th 1941 9.30pm OLW, Home to RCW, HMS *Royal Arthur*

"We have just heard the news – Japan seems to be breaking out actively[76] – wonder what the action of America will be. Wondering all the time what kind of a journey you have and if the trains are warm. Shall be glad to hear from you. Have just sent John a line giving all the details of the weekend and telling him how much we wished he could have been here too... Hope J*{S}* enjoyed herself and reached home safely. Next time there is no reason why she cannot stay the night. Am having the large bedroom blacked out. They are coming to measure up Tuesday... A fellow named W... – at Skegness may come & make your acquaintance. He is the son of one of my Volunteers working in the Borough Restaurant at Hackbridge... "

Dec 10th 1941 RCW, *Royal Arthur* to Home

"Just to tell you that I'm definitely moving to Shotley on Friday morning – so don't write anything to me here after you receive this..."

Dec 14th 1941 RCW, Mess 33, HMS *Ganges*, Shotley, Suffolk to Home

"I arrived down here at 7 o'clock on Friday night – after leaving Skegness at 8 a.m. – fancy nearly 12 hours to come not more than 100 miles. This establishment is right overlooking Harwich Harbour at present quite full of different ships and is 9 miles or 1/6 return bus fare from Ipswich... "

---

[76] Attack on Pearl Harbour on morning of Dec 7th 1941. Dec 8th US declared war on Japan.

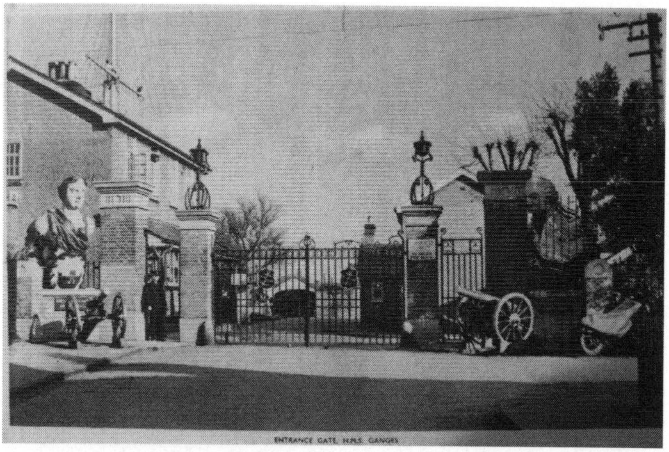

ENTRANCE GATE, H.M.S. GANGES

BOYS' MESS, H.M.S. GANGES

"ANNEXE," H.M.S. GANGES

Fig 23 Four postcards of HMS Ganges, Shotley belonging to RCW: Entrance, Boys Mess, Parade Ground

Dec 14th 1941

"... I went there [Ipswich] yesterday afternoon. It's a fine town – rather larger I should say than Croydon – shops appeared full of Xmas goods and literally seething... By the way there is no chance of my being home for the 25th... I have come into this mess with one of the fellows from Skegness. We have struck very lucky indeed as 33 is renowned to be the best in the place... We have a very excellent wireless, electric iron, plenty of hot water – everything is incredibly clean – far different story from *Royal Arthur*... There's a parquet floor – like glass and iron beds (exactly like school). Food so far has been quite decent. The fellows – all under 20 are a good natured lot (there are 50 in the Mess) & very helpful – but all kinds you can guess... They all seem to be writing Christmas cards or letters at the moment and are very subdued as they were inoculated yesterday... They have only been in the navy 4 weeks so I'm in comparison quite an old stager... What does Daddy think about the Japanese... - the loss of those 2 ships was certainly a heavy blow it also looks as if America might have been asleep too. It's high time they were woken up though - I can't see they would have ever come in before – unless attacked – Could M send me a face flannel... "

Dec 17th 1941 OLW, Home to RCW, HMS *Ganges*

"... The loss of those two ships was a great catastrophe – someone slipped up... Aid to Russia Day is going well – Banked £290 today and still have 90 tins to open... "

Dec 17th 1941 RCW, HMS *Ganges* to Home

"... we have to arise at 6 a.m. and 6.30-7.15 is spent in clearing up the mess. The instruction itself is far better as they have plenty of the necessary apparatus which makes it the more interesting. We go rowing in Harwich harbour – which is quite a rendezvous for destroyers etc and they have 2 complete batteries of 4 and 6 inch guns which the class is just starting on – That's called heavy gunnery – I've been fortunate in that the class has just finished all its preliminary rifle-training and drill – so I shan't have to go through with all that again. The food situation is the fly in the ointment – very stingy quantities and only 2 canteens for something like 3000 fellows – There never seems to be any chocolate at all - The most I've been able to get each day is 2 bullet like rock-buns – and after a tea consisting of <u>one</u> slice of bread and butter and either jam or a very small cake – it doesn't seem to me good enough... I shall be going to Ipswich on Friday – (there's apparently nothing at Harwich) – as I haven't been out of the camp this week. By the way we don't have anything like so much evening leave here – which is probably just as well since Ipswich is 9 miles away..."

Dec 21st 1941 RCW, HMS *Ganges* to Home

"What a wonderful Christmas parcel – thank you all very much - I thought John's 3 in one eating set one of the most original things I've ever seen – you've no idea how useful it will be later on and besides, it's a great point to have ones own knife, fork etc. How on earth did Mummie manage the Turkish Delight?... Auntie *{Terese}* also sent me some chocolate which I thought very decent. Last night I had a letter from Sir W *{his godfather}* with the 'usual' seasonal contribution enclosed... Later on this afternoon we are going to set to and decorate; each mess has been given 30/- of paper decorations – so that should help to brighten things up a bit. The 25th itself I understand is to be an absolutely free one, and we are, I believe, being allowed to stay in bed until 7.30. To answer a question of Ms

11 people including myself came from Skegness, but only 2 of us came into '33'. Last night however 2 more followed... "

Dec 21st 1941 CEW, Home to RCW, HMS *Ganges*

"... Pity you can't clear up the 'Jap' schmozzle for me – it has knocked the markets to billy-ho again – just when things seem to be mending... John looks fit – bigger and heavier without doubt... Your lady friend *{JS}* sent the cuttings of Peterboro along – very good – looks as though you were sulking at not being the Admiral! But anyway you looked miles better for your first 6 weeks of it when you came home... Well, boy, don't paint Ipswich red on the Great Day, or eat 15 suppers, or buy a yellow and green tie, or get 'lit up' or anything of that sort – rather let us all offer our thanks that we're all still here safe, well and unharmed, and a silent little prayer that by next Christmas we may all be re-united... "

Dec 25th 1941 RCW, HMS *Ganges* to Home

"... They have made a big effort here to conjure up the spirit of Christmas, in the way of decorations, free cigarettes, free beer, various entertainments... but it's hardly like being at home. I listened to the King's speech this afternoon – thought the end was much in Churchill's style... since that last word I have spent 1 hour in the shelters, air raid, no sound or sign though... "

Dec 31st 1941 RCW, HMS *Ganges* to Home

"... I have been on the water several days this week and all this afternoon was steering a steam-boat around Harwich! – This morning we were rowing and sailing!! By the way I ought perhaps to mention I shall be leaving here in just under a month – sooner than I expected – that of course does not mean I shall be going straight to sea – it might be another month or two at my base which is Portsmouth... Poor cousin Peter I most certainly wouldn't like to be in his shoes – Poland of all places – ought I to write to Mablethorpe?... "

1942

Jan 1st 1942 JRW, Home to RCW, HMS *Ganges*

"I daresay you are as excited as I am about the bike, so as there is no news whatsoever to report, I will proceed with a few details: - ... a BSA, 1934 (fig 24), 150 cc. and therefore <u>not</u> fast! Anyway it does at least look like a real motorbike and although it is low powered is just as big and heavy as the Scott... due to the innumerable accessories such as lights, batteries, electric horn etc... and is even complete with amp-metre inset in the headlamp which has blackout master all complete with bright and dips switch... It also has a good speedometer... On the whole I think it quite a decent little bike... So it awaits your judgment!... PS We've just heard from J*{S}* that she has managed to get seats for "Gangway"... ought to be very good... PPSS Mummie invited J*{S}* to stay on Sat night after the show but don't say anything in your letter here yet – M is paving the way with Daddy!"

Jan 6th 1942 JRW, Home to RCW, HMS *Ganges*

"... There's no more to say except to wish you a pleasant journey, (if that's possible on the British Railways) and let you know we are all looking forward to Friday and preparing for 11 days of real enjoyment... "

Feb 4th 1942 RCW, Portsmouth Mess 3G, Royal Naval Barracks (RNB) *{*HMS *Victory}* to Home

"I have just had some supper and am sitting in the writing-room of what was the Savoy Hotel, Southsea – it's now been taken over by the British Sailor's Society but still retains much of its former glory! Southsea is about 10 minutes bus ride from Portsmouth and this place is well worth it. This is my first night off (4.30 till 7.30 morning) but I'm returning to RNB after this. (As a matter of fact it's one shilling to sleep here per night with clean sheets – so it's not exactly extortionate). Last night I was on A.R.P. *{Air Raid Precautions}* duty but as there was no alert I slept all night in a bunk in a shelter exactly like our cellar but don't worry it <u>wasn't</u> damp. It snowed last night but is now raining hard and has turned rather warmer. I am doing a signals course – which ought to prove useful to me later but there's plenty of variety thrown in i.e. swimming yesterday afternoon (indoor bath very warm)… " *{p2 of letter missing}*

Fig 24 JRW on the motorbike in Home Guard uniform with Lee Enfield on his back at home!

Feb 7th 1942 RCW, RNB Portsmouth to JRW, Charterhouse

"… This is a pretty terrible hole for the most part – although the food is excellent which makes up for a lot. The rest of the time seems to be spent falling in and off the parade – we spent 3 hours on Friday in best suits for commanders inspection – bitterly cold too and we are not allowed to wear gloves. But I expect you know all about the cold though as Portsmouth isn't really so far from Godalming. I have no idea how long I shall be here as some people stay months others only a few days. As a matter of fact there has been a slight rumour that I shall be off shortly however best just wait and see. Should I go suddenly though – whenever you're home I hope you'll be able to look up J*{S}* occasionally – letters are so slow from ships and usually one receives them in bunches at rather long intervals. I hope that by the time you get home at the end of the term you will have decided something about your future for certain – I don't think its advisable to keep Daddy hanging about do you? By the way do you know I had another letter from V but for heaven sake – don't mention it, should you see J*{S}*... – as I don't think I'll answer it – otherwise I can't see it will ever cease!... "

Feb 17th 1942 RCW, on train *{presumably heading for HMS Charlestown – see Summary of Service}*, to Home

"I'm writing this note on the train bound for Grimsby – there are just three of us going – all were with me at Skegness – so I know them well – and that I think is a good thing. I had very little time in London so I'm afraid I was not able to 'make' Dorlands *{Advertising Agency W1}* to see Daddy – but guess he will understand. I will write as often as possible – in my case I believe the opportunities should be fairly good both for sending & receiving – however it remains to be seen - anyway I'm intending to post this at Peterborough... Cheerio then and don't worry"

Feb 21st 1942 RCW, Mess 4 HMS *Charlestown* (see Fig 3) to Home (Stamped "RECEIVED FROM HM SHIPS")

"... I'm afraid it will take me some time before I become an expert at letter writing nowadays as there are so many things I must not mention – however I know for the time being that it will suffice you to know that I am well - I am with a very decent crowd of fellows and I find them most helpful as things seem so different to those one learns in training. I hope you won't mind the pencil but ink is rather apt to get knocked over – things being rather cramped... Cheerio – don't worry – and all the best Much Love Dick"

April 5th 1942 JS, Gerrards Cross to RCW, Mess 4 HMS *Charlestown* c/o GPO, London

"Happy Easter darling wherever you are!... I've been wondering what it is like with you – whether it is horribly rough (the sea I mean) and if you have quite overcome sea sickness… Good Friday was much the same as any other day with me, but in the shop it was just like Hampstead Heath on a Bank Holiday! Whole families came in complete with pram, ice cream cornets & peanuts & we took over £4000 in cash!… " (page 2 of letter missing)

April 9th 1942 (RCW's birthday) JS, Oxford St W1 to HMS *Charlestown*

"What a beastly day for your birthday… I've no doubt I could wait years & years if you were waiting too, not that I would enjoy the waiting but I would do it, because I still reckon you are worth it!… A *{family friend}* left last Friday & asked to be remembered to you… "

April 15th 1942 RCW, HMS *Charlestown* to Home (stamped RECEIVED FROM HM SHIPS and PASSED BY CENSOR)

"… Auntie Terese & Grandma sent me 16/-… When I rang Daddy the other day – I had just come from a long walk through the most beautiful scenery imaginable. I have managed quite a few recently. I have also revisited the two old ladies with the huge house & butler – I was able to have an excellent hot bath followed by a lounge supper – I am apparently very welcome whenever in the vicinity… What price the "budget" I am afraid that as yet I have been unable to glean much information – except that they seem unable to 'soak' the rich man any more… Meanwhile yours truly plugs on at 20/- or so per week… I don't like the look of things out East at all besides a failure of agreement with India, the wretched Japs seem to soak us completely whenever we meet them – are the 5% Bonds at nil yet? They ought to be!… There is no need to worry about my end – so Cheerio… "

April 15th 1942 JS, 6.45pm, St James Park, London to RCW, HMS *Charlestown*

"… the park is becoming more mutilated every time I see it. Huts & barbed wire seem to be springing up everywhere. They have taken all the iron palings down that used to line the Mall & keep such as us out after closing time – remember darling?...D.H.E.'s H.G. platoon is going strong… They are having an exercise over the week-end lasting 25 hours & have got to exist on their iron-rations. I'm on duty Sat to Sun morning, so I hope they won't get too rough or I may be kept busy!... I wonder where you are... "

April 19th 1942 JS, 10.45 am on train Victoria to Wallington to RCW, HMS *Charlestown*

"I've been on fire watch all night & have had hardly any sleep. The Home Guard have been on a long exercise... 2 hours... There are about 60 of them and they are existing on iron rations & doing all their own cooking etc. You can imagine what their hobnailed boots sound like in that Basement *{presumably basement of store in Oxford St where she worked}*. Miss J... was the other nurse on with me & we were commandeered by the Platoon Commander... so we had to keep on the Q.V. all night in case we were wanted but all that had to be done was to dress a carbuncle on a Home Guarder's arm!... "

April 29th 1942 RCW, Glasgow to Home telegram

"Arrived safely writing Dick"

April 30th 1942 JS, The Flat, London to RCW, HMS *Charlestown*

"... I am so glad you enjoyed those few days too... wonderful to have you home again... [May 1st] I'm writing this in the Hairdressing... I'm finishing this in the Cafeteria... "

May 2nd May (Saturday) RCW, HMS *Charlestown* to Home

"... I have had two afternoons & evenings in Glasgow which is only 30 minutes bus ride away. It is very like London and seems just as large and stuffy. There are some excellent shops. Lewis's is really fine and appears to be doing an enormous trade. I have never seen such a variety of stock in any London store especially with regard to food... Yesterday I went to Glasgow's Empire theatre to one of George Black's shows – Vera Lynn, Rawicz & Landauer[77] the latter were

---

[77] Rawicz and Landauer were an immensely popular piano duo team that performed from 1932 to 1970. They were initially based in Vienna, Austria, but moved to the United Kingdom in the early part of their career. They were known for their arrangements of popular classics...They escaped Nazi Europe in 1935 and moved to the United Kingdom with their wives, becoming favourites of the Prince of Wales (later King Edward VIII).[3] During World War II, like many people originally from Europe, they found themselves considered potential enemies and were interned on the Isle of Man. After release, they both became British subjects.

simply wonderful and brought the roof down… I slept at the Church of Scotland Club… I am doing 24 hours on 24 off and this gets a few hours extra leave. I don't believe we shall be here much longer but you will know by the fact the there will be no stamps on my letters. At present though the ship is practically in pieces, hundreds of dockers banging and drilling all day long… "

May 3rd 1942 JS, Oxford St, W1 to RCW HMS *Charlestown*

"I'm writing to you in the Fire Watch room… Mr R is on duty with us tonight & I have just been having a further report on his infant – He thinks she is perfect, his wife a marvel & everything in the garden is lovely! Thank heaven there are still some such simple souls walking about on this earth!… The Duty team have just started arriving – they don't have to report until 9.30pm now. Do you remember darling how we used to go out in the evening & have supper & go for a walk & the incident of the bad temper & the hat?! I often think of that whenever I go up Portland Place & have to grin because I must have looked the funniest sight out!… "

May 10th 1942 RCW, HMS *Charlestown* to Home

"… The village were just in the middle of the opening of their War Weapons Week – target no specified amount; one or two flags – and a march past lasting precisely two minutes – then all was over and everybody simply faded into oblivion. Has Daddy ever been to Glasgow… it differs little there are plenty of shops but they seem to be better stocked than down south. One day I happened to be in Glasgow… they were holding their annual May Day Procession – it's a sort of trades union affair – banners, brass bands etc… the nearest thing I've seen to the Coronation. The place I thought was very 'Red' and standing in the crowd it was advisable to keep one's mouth shut. Did I tell you Harrods have sent my underwear 17/6 the lot… "

May 19th 1942 RCW, HMS *Charlestown* to Home

"… In Glasgow where we are for a few days once again… I had an excellent bath there [at the Church of Scotland Club]… I am allowed off (board) every other night it's as well I think to make the most of it

---

Extracted from: http://en.wikipedia.org/wiki/Rawicz_and_Landauer (http://creativecommons.org/licenses/by-sa/3.0/)

as it is only very rarely we see any decent sized place at all. I managed to hear most of Churchill's speech the other Sunday and thought it rather encouraging – events at present too I believe point in that direction – the Russians hold the balance and provided we can keep up the supplies I see no reason why they shouldn't 'lick' Germany in the long run. Hitler seems to be throwing in such a lot now and without impression it would appear. We hope it's that way at any rate. The whole business has gone on long enough. But even then after effects may be worse still. I have been doing a great deal of painting recently [on the ship] so when you're at a few square feet in the house – remember you do not stand alone!!... "

May 29th 1942 from RCW, HMS *Charlestown* (censor, no stamp) to Home

"I fear this will only be a terribly short note but if I say 'business' has had to take preference you will doubtless be able to understand my short coming... I have had one stroke of misfortune – the loss of my post office book... "

May 31st 1942 RCW, HMS *Charlestown* to OLW, The Town Hall Wallington

"... I am sending this line to the town hall as it is to get your opinion first. Do you think that Daddy would ever fall in with the idea of my having a few days holiday with J*{S}*? Frankly I can't possibly think he would... of course the idea itself has at present no bottom as I have not the least knowledge of when I should be home again... In any case if you believe D would be dead against the idea I will of course pack it up and if you believed that it be so, I would rather you did not mention it all – as I am of the opinion he is perhaps a little concerned over things as they are... "

June 9th 1942 RCW, HMS *Charlestown* to Home

"... As to your question about my next leave firstly I could not tell you if I knew – secondly I have no more idea than you when it will be... "

June 17th 1942 RCW, Glasgow to Home

"Here's a line to let you know how much I enjoyed my 72 hours even though it passed so quickly. When I reached Euston an hour and a half before the train was due to leave it was already packed! Not even a spare sleeper and you can guess I had visions of nine hours or so in the corridor. However there was a special military train on the next platform – marked 'not for public use' and after much wangling I persuaded the inspector to let me travel on it. I had the whole of one seat for myself! And I was therefore able to stretch out and get some sleep – I arrived back at five minutes to eight – all the other London people were late – due to the 9.15 coming in 90 minutes after time. The train I was on took preference and held it up... Last night I went to the Empire Variety – saw Charlie Kunz – he certainly is a master – Beryl Orde the radio impersonator... PS Cold improving, don't worry"

June 28th 1942 RCW, Glasgow to Home

"I am afraid that try as I did I was quite unable to phone from Euston the other night – I simply could not get the operator by dialling 0 which is a necessary move to contact a non-automatic exchange – However the ride went off very well indeed – I was sound asleep from 10.30 to 6 and eventually reached Glasgow at 7. There were 4 little beds in each compartment and the other three occupants were an army captain on leave and a commander and his wife (newly married I should say!). They were all three very affable – something I felt rather dubious about on seeing them and considering I was a mere rating!!... I have had two trips into the town since I returned just a visit to a cinema & a spot of supper, bath & bed... This morning I went to Church... I have read todays newspapers it would appear that we are unable to check them in Africa and at that rate things may be looking pretty black shortly... Cheerio then... "

July 5th 1942 RCW, HMS *Charlestown* to Home

"... precious little news – Well I mean by that news that I can write about. However I have once again run into some of my former friends at Skegness & Ganges... quite a few enjoyable hours ashore with them... I think that I am better for the present way of life – physically at any rate. Mentally I have my doubts one does not have the opportunity for clear thinking of all that I believe is necessary in that respect – the edge seems to be dulled if you can understand my meaning... "

July 15th 1942 RCW, HMS *Charlestown* to Home

"... I am glad to know that the fish arrived safely and that you were able to guess the sender – as a matter of fact I am tomorrow despatching another small parcel of 'eats' and hope that they too will 'make' Wallington... I am well and kicking although could do with some better weather – the places I have been seem to have no summer as I have been accustomed to know it... I can't say I like the way things are blowing in Russia but resign myself to thinking that there is little more I can do about it... "

July 27th 1942 OLW, Home to RCW, HMS *Charlestown*

"... upset not to get a letter off to you on Sunday last – was thoroughly disorganised. First of all John was on Home Guard Manoeuvres all night Saturday arriving here at 4am Sunday – and where do you think these operations took place – on the Beddington Sewerage Farm. Can you imagine John's disgust. In the evening there was a parade of all the Youth Organisations preceded by a massed service in the Parish Church Sea Cadets, Sea Scouts, Girls Training Corps, Air Cadets, Army Cadets, Guides & Scouts... the Sea Cadets were magnificent... To me they all looked like 'my little Richard'... we have lived in the height of luxury on the contents of the parcel which arrived in perfect condition on Saturday morning. The c...m (sic) was a glorious companion to the last of the season's raspberries. As for the rest will leave you to imagine... "

July 30th 1942 RCW, HMS *Charlestown* (censor, no stamp) to Home

"Here I am again in the best of spirits and hope you are too... I have had a letter from D*{B, friend from home}* – he says he saw the ship (this one) some weeks ago but there was no time to get a signal across – still he appears to be enjoying life although it should not be difficult knowing the standard of living. I have also heard from Uncle Ted *{married to Terese, OLW's sister}*... mentions he would very much like me to pay Cinderford a visit – I myself would certainly like one or two days down there... I hope... John has completely recovered... I myself am now about to have a haircut by the one and only fellow on board capable of doing the job – so Cheerio... "

Aug 7th 1942 RCW, HMS *Charlestown* at sea to Home

"... I have passed my first selection board and should be leaving the ship shortly. It is not nearly such a stiff one as the next (The Admiralty one) but it is at least another step nearer – and I am quite pleased with things generally. My friend on board was not so fortunate "lacking in confidence" he was told and has to do further sea time before coming up again before the board. ... I don't like the sound of the news at all – unless of course the Russians are letting them advance so much on purpose – I should hardly think so though... "

Aug 10th 1942 V *{friend}*, Cinderford, Glos to RCW, HMS Charlestown

"At the moment life here is very hectic for the staff *{Hospital at Longford}* is now cut down to ½ its size so we're very rushed but we don't mind it will help to get this beastly war over. We've had several letters recently from my bro' Ken who as I expect you know is a PoW & he said he was feeling fit & well & is now wearing a pair of shorts he made himself... & socks & boots so it must be pretty warm out there... I do hope I shall hear from you again <u>soon</u> - not forgetting the photo you promised me... "

Aug 12th 1942 OLW, Home to RCW, HMS *Charlestown*

"... Congratulations on having passed the first selection board and as you say it's just another step nearer. So sorry for your friend... The news is anything but encouraging. However my faith is strong in spite of the setbacks. May be, or at least, I trust our Leaders see farther ahead than the public are allowed to. Anyway they cannot always say all they would like to... KO is going in the A.T.S. Friday week... she is quite thrilled at the prospect. She was in to see me on Sunday night and told me this in great secrecy. PO and his girl have parted... the girl's mother talked of marriage – after the war – put the wind up P – writes frantic letter breaking it all off – she writes asking for return of all the presents she had given him, all the comforts, worn or not worn saying they would do for the next fellow!!!... It's compulsory firewatching for women up to 45... "

Aug 14th 1942 JS, The Flat to RCW, HMS *Charlestown* redirected to HMS *King Alfred II*, Hove, Sussex – official move there Nov 15th 1942.

Aug 15th 1942 RCW to Home Telegram

"Hope to be home for night Saturday with friend Dick"

Sept 3rd 1942 R *{friend}* (as of HMS Titania,[78] c/o GPO) to RCW, HMS *King Alfred {following meeting up on a period of leave}*

"... back on board at about two o'clock Sunday morning after the usual hectic journey. Travelling nowadays is a pretty grim business... The weather, as could only be expected, simply beggars description. And there are actually human beings who have lived in this climate all their lives, and done nothing about it... Write and tell me how you get on at K.A. *{King Alfred}...* "

Sept 13th 1942 RCW, Home to JRW, Cockburn Hotel Edinburgh

"Passed Admiralty Board on Friday – home this weekend and hope to be next as well. Living in very comfortable billet at Hove... PS M.B. Engine looks ok"

Sept 29th 1942 JS to RCW, Frobisher Division, HMS *King Alfred* [79], Shoreham by Sea

"... Sunday evening... Shall we say 6.20 pm Victoria under the clock as last time?... Lancing certainly sounds pretty good - & it must be a most agreeable change after HMS *Charlestown*. Don't be silly of course I am interested in anything you can tell me about the place or what you do. I just don't ask questions because I'm never quite sure what you are supposed to tell me and what you are not... "

Oct 5th 1942 JS, Oxford St, W1 to RCW, HMS *King Alfred* (L)

"So far so good – but at the moment the medical is the decisive factor... told I was ideally suited for the job which appears to be very varied – even to doing night work – still who cares!... I was interviewed by a girl who used to be on duty with me at the Middlesex Hospital First Aid Post at the beginning of the war – who is now an officer in the WRMS of some rank or other... "

---

[78] Submarine depot ship (http://home.cogeco.ca/~gchalcraft/sm/depot.html)

[79] The three elements of 'King Alfred' evidently became identified by a location letter instead of the usual suffix 'II' or 'III'; the main headquarters site in Hove was referred to as both 'King Alfred' and 'King Alfred (H)', Lancing as 'King Alfred (L')', and Mowden 'King Alfred (M)'. (http://www.royalnavyresearcharchive.org.uk)

Oct 10th 1942 DB *{friend from home}* HMS *Bicester* [80] to RCW, HMS *King Alfred*

"... Have you made any choice as to what you're going to do after K.A. For Gods sake keep out of Tank Landing Craft. Of course if I was you I'd say destroyers at once but maybe the sea doesn't appeal to you all that much... I find shore life far too hectic these days and three or four days in harbour and I'm quite ready to go to sea again. We've been having some colossal parties of late, several of them onboard... "

Nov 10th 1942 CEW, Home to RCW "Cadet Rating R Wiles", Frobisher Div, HMS *King Alfred*

"... The news seems almost too good to be true [81] – I can't yet bring myself to break windows and chuck my hat in the air – but may be that's coming. Anyway God bless you and be cheered by what the New Zealanders said!"

Nov 19th 1942 Pro Wren JS, WRMS Depot, The Ridgway, Mill Hill, London NW7 to RCW, HMS *King Alfred*

"... We've had supper & now are waiting for medicals at 7.45pm... this place it's so large & crowded & women women everywhere over 800 of them... a new building & nothing looks properly finished... "

Nov 20th 1942 CEW, Home to RCW, HMS *King Alfred*

"Dear Sub Lieutenant... John... is keeping the most ungodly hours... the other morning he returned at 6am from Home Guard watch, chilled to the bone. M *{OLW}* has a violent cold and keeps prowling out to 'Prisoner of War' meetings and heaven knows what... Congratulations on your promotion and my every good wish for your continued health & happiness. I am not forgetful of the hint I gave you concerning certain little obligations born of your new status – I mean obligations of mine. All in due time! Thine – Dad"

Nov 27th 1942 V, Cinderford, Glos to RCW, HMS *King Alfred*

---

[80] Escort destroyer: NW Approaches & Gibraltar around this time. (http://www.naval-history.net/xGM-Chrono-10DE-Bicester.htm)
[81] Victory at El Alamein Nov 5th 1942 presumably

"... Yes I admit I was a little unhappy when I was with you – the reason being that I was of course upset at your going back & because of the short time we were together – I would have given anything to have spent the whole of your leave with you & to think we only had a few hrs!! I'm sorry... I must have spoilt your leave... "

Dec 13th 1942 CEW, Dorland Advertising Ltd to RCW, on way to ship

"... Buckingham Palace Road was nearly empty, a few stragglers stood round the Palace railings watching a noisy sergeant-major bellowing at some Guards paraded on the forecourt. Then up through Ambassador's Court with none but a sentry, guarding nothing against nobody, up St James' Street with only a stray soldier or two in sight, then wheeling into Jermyn Street, past the only open shop, a poor little café, fly blown bottles of coloured drinks... in the window, past the dreadful spectre of skeletoned St James' Church, only my footfall sounding, till, on the instant reminding me of the sham of this strange peace, the far-off boom of heavy gunfire, roaring dully every thirty seconds of so, still booming as I write at this untidy desk.

Perhaps it was that that made the queue of waiting hobs grow suddenly unimportant, that made it seem a better idea that I should spend a happier hour, on paper chatting with you, without correction, intrusion, interruption... For it just may be, as this new chapter opens on your way to your hidden destination and to adventures and experiences and may be trials equally unknown, that you will be glad of a few words from an old yet devoted codger which may help to smooth your way and even light your path.

So far you have done well; so far the road has been bravely and wisely travelled; so far you have, I know, sidetracked or demolished the lions (or the foxes) in your path. From now on the journey may perhaps be more comfortable in some ways but be sure it will be trickier, more puzzling, less easy. You will have abler critics; you will be weighed in the balance of perhaps richer, more high-brow, more reckless, more impressive and seemingly more enviable companions. How to hold your own among them? Not certainly, by aping them. Not by any pose, pretence or affectation - nothing shows what you are quicker. Not by 'currying favour'. Not by trying to be a dozen kinds of people at once, not by sailing with every wind, not by striving come what may to be 'popular'. No but you may hold your own, more than hold your own, in whatever company or circumstance by being yourself, by being guided and counselled by the promptings of your conscience and your character. 'Stand firmly on your two legs' says Emerson 'and in the end the world, the sneering, jeering, fearing world, will admire and respect you.' That, Dick, is true; everlastingly true; bear it in mind.

Of what the old women call 'temptation' I'm sure you'll need neither my information nor my warning. Temptations will come along all right, 'in single spies and in battalions', perhaps more insidious, more inviting, more 'commonly accepted' than ever. Once let them overcome you and regret, remorse, and worse will go on exacting their mounting misery as long as life lasts. That, dear lad, is no 'goody-goody' preaching; it's brass-tacks common sense – undeniable, irrefutable, though so many of us have had to learn it by experience; having had no guidance, nor frank and honest telling, only hints and whisperings and wicked silence. So, travelling through the all-prevailing seas of muck, some naturally stuck to be scraped off in disillusion, unhappiness, despair.

Think beforehand not after. Pass these matters through the sieve of your conscience, your character, your faith and hope and belief in the promises and commandments of the only Benefactor who remains to watch our troubled lives, and all the dross and muck and misery will remain safely behind, in the sieve.

Not for worlds would I be thought to 'preach'. I speak of nothing but what the long and hard and often lonely years have taught me. It is not the borrowings from books, not the bleak jabbering of 'old women': it is the uncompromising and often cruel teaching encountered by an old fellow who at seven years old found himself, fatherless, flung straight into 'life'.

But of course there's the sunnier side; the days of adventure; the ever-new delight of fresh scenes, fresh people; the travel, the change of grub and habitation and duty, the ever-growing horizon of your days.

There you have me beat, hands down. For I've been just a human shuttle, to and fro in little railway trains, among the little people, home-office, office-home, for more than twice the years that you have so far lived! Boy, you can afford to patronise me by all such measurements. Some success, may be, but you may well laugh at its silly narrowness and I think sometimes I ought to laugh with you. Only, think kindly of my start, my handicaps, my opportunities compared with your own. It wasn't a case of making the most of my 'old school tie'; but rather of making something out of life without a tie at all! Lastly, as old W *{RCW's godfather}* said (though I don't go the whole way with him) take care of your finances. Work out a little plan for your expenditures and watch that plan! It may be 'fine' to be 'open-handed' but it's damn foolish to risk embarrassment or debt. 'Frittering' on this and that mounts to the very devil before you know where you are. Watch it boy; don't be mean; but watch it.

Now you must be far on your journey – tired I'm sure of train and me. But let me once more wish you well; you'll be forever in my thoughts and prayers, If I can help do please let me know, not as the old Dad, but rather, I hope, as an old and devoted pal. And whatever the days-to-be may hold, hold up your head and heart, keep smiling, with your faith in God and in those who love you, unimpaired and Happiness be yours, all your days. Your devoted Dad. [PS] Beginning January 1st I shall pay into your Deposit Account monthly £4.3.4, being one twelfth of £50 a year, as promised, and I enclose a note for pocket money on your journey. D"

Dec 14th 1942 RCW, HMS *Helder*[82] (see Fig 4) to Home

"Well I'm more or less settled in my new surroundings together with

---

[82] HMS *Helder* ~Function - Naval training, afloat and ashore, for officers and crews of minor landing craft. Brightlingsea. Base was commissioned on 5/4/42 and paid off on 30/9/44. Later, as RN Camp St Osyth, it was used as accommodation for Naval raiding parties. Other information - Up to 1/7/43 officers for marine landing craft were supplied by the training establishment *HMS King Alfred* at Hove where they entered as ratings, and following training, graduated as officers... The first 4 weeks were essentially on naval aspects and the remaining 2 in working with the military. During this phase flotillas of small landing craft were formed and allocated to Combined Operations bases where further training of formed flotillas was undertaken. Pending allocation to Force Commanders, formed flotillas could be attached to Combined Training Centres for work with the military. (from http://www.combinedops.com/Training%20EST%20UK.htm#HMS%20Helder)

four of the fellows who came down with me – for obvious reasons I am unable to say what I'm doing but let it suffice for now to tell you that it's very interesting work. Food is fairly good – better than K.A. at any rate. For John's benefit tell him... to write off about that matter I went to London for – at once. There is a present demand! Hope that's quite clear -... Cheerio for the present – don't worry... "

Dec 28th 1942 RCW, HMS *Helder* to home

"... a line to let you know that I arrived back safely at about nine last night... "

1943

Jan 4th 1943 Wren JS, WRNS Depot, Mill Hill NW7 to RCW HMS *Helder*

"… I had been wondering what had happened to you & if you had already made a move. I couldn't understand why you hadn't phoned me at home over Christmas – I should so much like to have spoken to you, but I expect you had your reasons. Thank you ever so much, dear, for your telegram… "

Jan 8th or 9th 1943 RCW, 2 pm Edinburgh to Home

"Best wishes from Princes's St, Edinburgh – just had breakfast at ?North British (arrived 1 hour ago – on the move again in 30 minutes). Send you address later."

Jan 11th 1943 RCW, Inverary, Argyllshire to OLW, Home

"… Have just forwarded one pair of black shoes to you – Will you have them heeled as soon as possible preferably 'rubber quarters' but doesn't matter. Can't get anything done of that nature here… Also I wonder if you have remembered my suit question for Mr Lee. If not can you proceed forthwith and ask him if it can be done in the next 10 days. I am hoping to come on 7 days leave Saturday week but of course nothing definite… Conditions here are the worst I've ever experienced – shan't be sorry to leave… PS I want a complete ring on my sleeves instead of the ½ as at present. Understood?"

Jan 12th 1943 CEW, Office to S/L RCW, Inverary, Argyllshire

"… NEWS ITEMS GL *{family friend}* dead… was to be married in February… she was 26. Complained of a headache after a day's driving, went to lie down and died in her sleep… it's unbelievable. John's Registration. He registered for the Army. This is why. I saw P. & also the Chairman of the Film Co. They said the Army was the only service with its own organised Film Unit (at Wembley). The C/O was requiring a camera assistant and as soon as John was in the Army they would 'claim' him for their assistant… They absolutely satisfied me that the Army offered the best chance of his getting into film work… And God bless you, boy, Thine Dad"

Jan 18th 1943 RCW, Inverary, Argyllshire to Home

"... I'm sorry the phone call was so indistinct last night it was most annoying as I had to book it three hours in advance – I was actually ringing from the George Hotel which was my headquarters for last night – (I was officer of the patrol) – the latter being for the purpose of maintaining law and order in the town (drunks etc) will tell you more though – I have just returned from a ten mile walk this afternoon. I went with a fellow to a tiny place called Furnace where, believe it or not, I was able to buy several 'torch batteries' and have a very excellent 'Scottish tea'... I'm hoping to travel home at the end of the week... In any case please don't forward me any more letters etc... I am posting a parcel of washing Monday... "

Jan 22nd 1943 V, Cinderford, Glos to RCW, Home

" Dearest... I do hope you will get some proper leave soon though you don't sound very hopeful about it, but it really is the only thing I have to look forward to... For my part I never go out... There is also the coming back in the blackout (from seeing a film) which I have been very jittery about doing since one of our girls was supposed to have been assaulted – her own fault I should imagine... "

Feb 9-12th 1943 Wren JS, WRNS Depot, Mill Hill NW7 posted Feb 13th

"You certainly do get around... I had an interview with our Chief Officer (3 rings)... and she said she was putting me forward to before the Selection Board... "

Feb 12th 1943 V, Cinderford, Glos to RCW, Home

"... I should love a photo... of you in (full length) uniform... You will probably say some swear words about me asking for one but as I'm not there to hear them I don't mind... "

Feb 17th 1943 RCW 126 Flotilla, HMS *Foliot* [83], Plymouth to OLW

" I arrived back yesterday morning at about 6.30am... secured corner seats, surprisingly few travellers considering the end of a 'weekend'...

---

[83] HMS Foliot I Function - landing craft accounting base...HMS Foliot III Function - holding base for Combined Ops personnel. Address and commissioning history - Bickleigh, Plymouth. Base was commissioned from 7/43 to 10/46. (http://www.combinedops.com/Training%20EST%20UK.htm)

exceedingly cold… ”

Feb 23rd 1943 RCW, Royal Naval Barracks, Devonport (on embossed headed paper) to Home

“… you will see I have moved, but it is for this week only in order to do a special course on ‘gas’. It is proving exceedingly interesting though a trifle fearsome! Best of all though are the living conditions – superb is the only word that can fairly describe them. The thought of returning to ‘Foliot’ at the end of the week gives me the ‘shudders’. The food just takes one right back to peace time and dinner in the evening (bow ties etc!) is enhanced by The Royal Marines Band playing from the balcony… I saw H’s *{Harrods}* profits – they certainly seem to have had a good year!!… PS Sitting opposite me also writing a letter is a ‘full blown’ admiral!!!”

March 5th 1943 RCW No address yet (post marked Plymouth) to OLW

“… just posted a parcel of dirty clothes – can you please get them done quickly and retain until you hear from me again. Had tea yesterday afternoon with the Dowdings – a kind of party with nobody under the rank of admiral except yours truly. They were very nice people though. I spent most of the time talking to Lady Astor on the matter of service canteens. She is Plymouth’s M.P. and what a live wire!… things very hectic at the moment – hope you are all well in spite of the recent ‘blitz’!… ”

March 5th 1943 Wren JS to RCW, 126 Flotilla HMS *Foliot* Plymouth, redirected to HMS *Prins Albert* c/o GPO London

“… I met your Mother last Wednesday after A’s *{family friends}* wedding… I have passed the Selection Board… last Monday & there was absolutely nothing in it, but I understand they put you through it all right at Greenwich!… I may be drafted straight from port to Greenwich & from Greenwich to “where you will”, so… ”

March 8th 1943 RCW, HMS *Prins Albert* (see Fig 5) (censor, no stamp) to Home

“I’m afraid this will have to be another quick one but at any rate long enough to let you have another new address. This kind you’ll remember only costs you a 1½d stamp!… Conditions are excellent on board also the food – so I've no complaints in that direction. I wonder if you would forward me my best suit – its rather essential now as my working one will doubtless become 'grubby'... PS I'm certainly glad to be out of those wretched camps!"

March 13th 1943 RCW to Home telegram

"Disregard yesterdays wire address same as before Dick"

March 26th 1943 RCW to Home with parcel from Roseneath (see Fig 4), Scotland

"Rather a lot I'm afraid and very dirty... PS I had to have that back tooth out about a week ago (cause of blood on some articles!)"

March 28th 1943 RCW, 126 flotilla Roseneath, Scotland to Home

"Well I have left the ship and am now actually residing at the above address – things here like the majority of these camps are pretty awful – especially after conditions in the ship which were wonderful. Fortunately my flotilla officer has an excellent little portable radiogram and some some equally good records. These help to brighten the generally dim outlook considerably... I'm afraid some of the articles are really black but you'll doubtless understand why. If I attempt another phone call – I'll make it later but it is so much easier to get through before six... I have no longer to spend nearly all my spare time censoring the flotilla's mail as I did on board – Believe me it was quite an education!! Some of the spelling!!... "

April 6th 1943 RCW, Roseneath, Scotland (OPENED BY EXAMINER 3668) to Home

"... I have one spark of bright news... as there is a probability of my getting a week's leave at the end of the month... of course nothing definite... I am very sorry to have left the ship. We were just beginning to get settled in and out we have to come. This is quite the worst place I have alighted as yet – food is simply appalling and organisation is well I'll say no more but leave it to the imagination!! But in spite of it all myself and the rest have been working very hard indeed – and no time at all for any pleasure. The weather has been awful... Well I'm Officer of the Day at the moment which means I'm responsible for a very large section of the camp and it's just time for me to make the nightly inspection 9pm so I shall have to be getting 'under way'... PS The queries and phone calls I've had today would make DHs *{DH Evans}* look funny! even in a sale!"

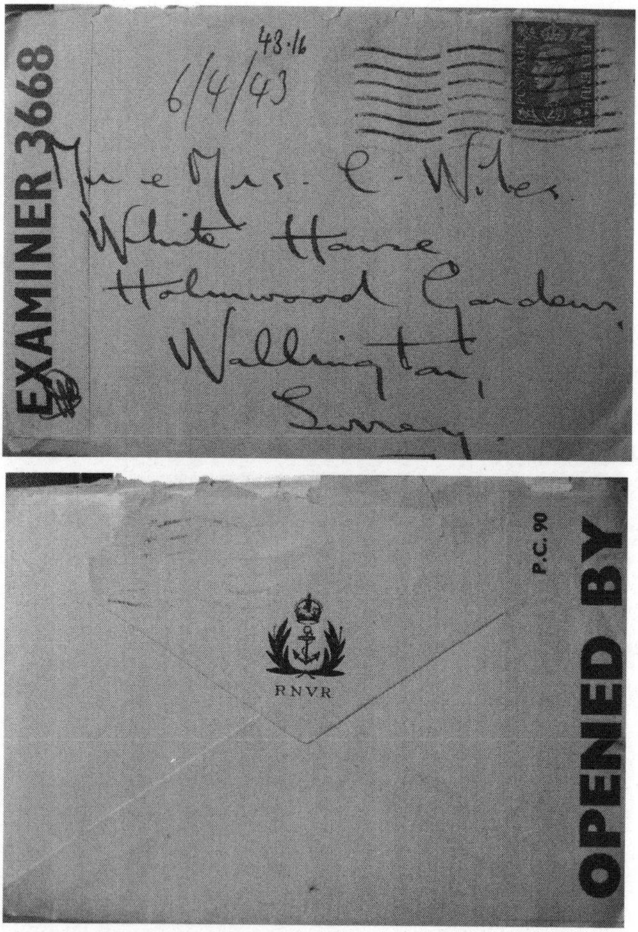

Fig 25 Example of censored letter which has been opened and resealed

April 6th 1943 CEW, Home to RCW, Roseneath, Scotland

"With all my heart I send best wishes for your 21st Birthday and for long long years of happiness ahead. In Kipling's brave phrase, you are now 'a man my son'... May you with His help 'steer your course true' "

April 24th 1943 RCW postcard of and from Tighnabruaich to Home

"Still going strong and hope to be home Sunday May 2nd... -isn't this place beautiful? – no time for more Cheerio"

April 25th 1943 RCW postcard of and from Tarbert to Home

"Here for this weekend – very bleak – weather simply atrocious! Looking forward to week home"

May 2nd 1943 Wren JS, Mess 8, HMS Wasp, Dover Kent to RCW, Royal Hotel, Tignabruaich redirected to PO Box 44 Roseneath Dumbartonshire (Censor/opened)

May 10th & May 17th 1943 RCW address as enclosed (126 flotilla Naval Party 869E c/o GPO)(opened by examiner 9389) to Home

"... my new address... train absolutely packed but I managed to secure a comfortable seat and slept most of the time... passed through large patches of country covered with snow... Well it doesn't seem like a week since I was at home but I suppose that hard work in the meanwhile accounts for that. The ship I am on is exceedingly comfortable and the food excellent – roast chicken for dinner tonight – plenty of fresh salads, white bread and eggs! Strangely enough my cabin is number nine! *{his lucky number}* And I share it with the officer from Richmond. I am enclosing 2 packets of blades for Daddy there seem to be quantities here... "

May 28th 1943 RCW to Home (top of letter cut off ?censor)

"Here I am again – this time having had more fresh air than ever before! Brown as a berry and altogether A.1... I literally haven't set foot ashore except for about 3 hours one Sunday afternoon. Oh there's one thing - will you pack up preferably in a wooden box my electric gramophone and send per passenger train to c/o Station Master GREENOCK"

June 26th 1943 RCW to JRW (address excised ?censor)

"... In a month's time you will receive a registered letter marked private and confidential. Do not open it but deposit it in a Bank (Westminster or Harrods) in your own name. Say nothing of it to Mummie and Daddy. The contents of this letter are simply a statement of what I wish to be done with my money and odds and ends I have – should anything happen to me. Now for Lord's sake don't get gloomy over this as the idea is simply a precaution – I hope it's all clear – leave in a bank – forget – say nothing O.K.? I wonder if you managed P's watch O.K. I haven't heard yet. *{second page missing}*"

June 27th 1943 CEW to RCW, 126 flotilla Naval Party No 869E

"... John, photoing in Belgrave Square... to Merton Park this morning for an hour... N's boy going on fairly well, three bullets still in him – three more months in hospital. The fuel people are now putting the screw on us agents again for ideas for the Autumn campaign – yelling for us to go down there at all hours and firing us appallingly foggy 'instructions' till we're all scrapping among ourselves as to what the h..l it is they really want. Oh the waste of time, brains and money – shocking."

July 3rd 1943 CEW to RCW, 126 flotilla Naval Party No 869E

"... Have at last arranged to earmark £200 a year for G *{CEW's Sister}* & Co and have sent her first £100. She is overwhelmed poor kid... I'm trying to nip down to Harrogate next Friday for a couple of days and explain things to them and see how G really is and how she's fixed – can't do it with letters... Young H... blew in yesterday – 3 weeks leave – but goodness he looked like he needed it. Never saw such a difference. He's ten years older, strained, thinned down and has lost his buoyancy completely. He didn't volunteer any reason... says he feels all right but 'done'... "

July 8th 1943 RCW, 126 flotilla Naval Party 869E to Home

"I expect that by the time you receive this you'll have guessed what I'm 'up to' – but that is as much as I can say. Naturally I have not heard from you at all and likewise you from me. I should guess though that John may have retired to the army!... I'm enjoying weather such as I've never experienced before – England simply doesn't have it and as a result I'm nearly black!... I'm hoping to run into DB *{friend}* sometime... I wrote and congratulated him on his decoration. I'm very glad that I brought my records along – they have proved most enjoyable both to myself and to many others besides... "

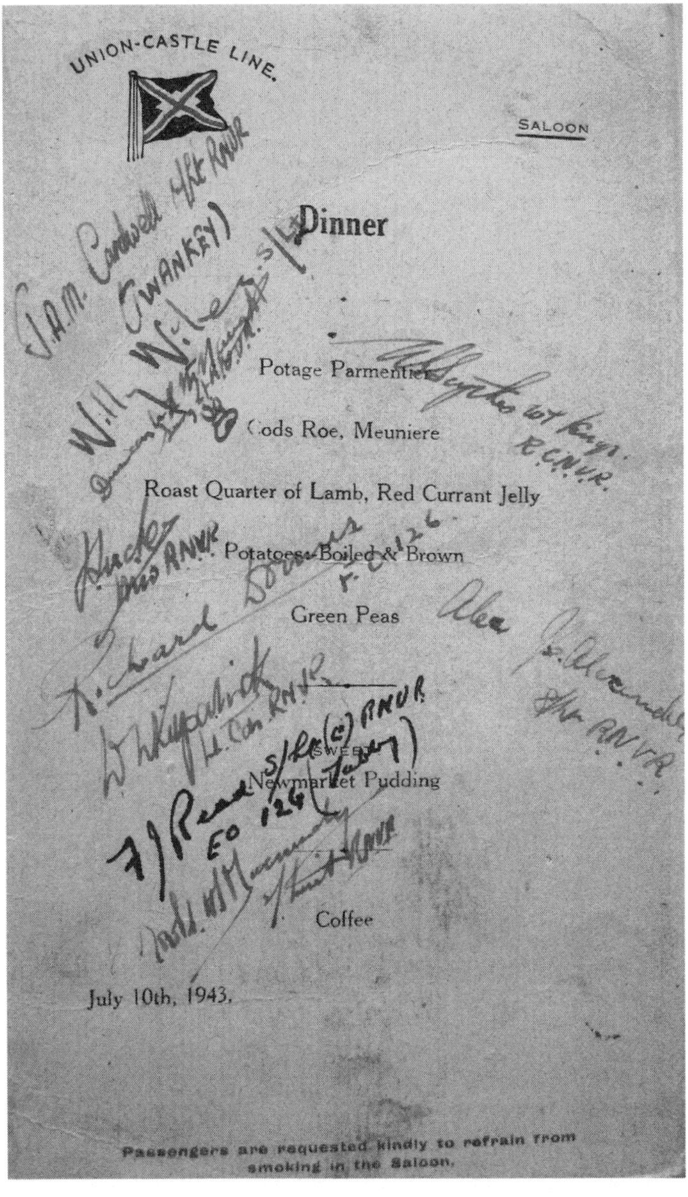

Fig 26 Signed menu from SS Llangibby Castle en route for N Africa / Sicily landings July 10th 1943 – note "Willy Wiles" near top

July 17th 1943 CEW to RCW, 126 flotilla Naval Party No 869E

"In view of the news in the papers my imagination about you and your whereabouts has – I think excusably – been running riot... All I hope and pray is that wherever you are and whatever may be your duties you are safe and well and gallant-hearted and happy and that we may soon have news of you. It seems half a life sitting at this desk these days with such mighty adventures going on all round – you are seeing and experiencing more things in a week than I've known in a lifetime. Trust in God, my dear lad, then you can 'keep smiling... ' "

July 24th 1943 CEW to RCW, 126 flotilla Naval Party No 869E

"... Mick *{nickname for OLW}* wants me to go to Town Hall lecture and Film on 'Scabies' Monday night – Regretfully declined!... We're still hoping for news. Great things seem to be happening fast... "

July 26th 1943 RCW via Greenock to JRW c/o Merton Park Studios, Merton Park, Surrey (Registered) two letters inside: a) to Mr & Mrs Charles Wiles: re disposal of assets, thanks, farewell b) to Miss K *{a friend}*

July 27th 1943 RCW, 126 Flotilla HMS *Hannibal* [84] airletter to Home

"Well, here I am safe and sound after – well you should be able to guess! Now residing ashore in Algiers – what a place boiling hot, millions of flies & mosquitoes as a result of which I'm stung to death... The fruit is about the only plentiful thing is delicious and cheap. I eat quite a lot of it. I understand D *{DB – friend}* may be home – have you seen him? I haven't received any letters now for nearly 6 weeks... There are several cinemas and American speaking films so there is some entertainment... please excuse the bluntness in this but I am only allowed one per week and as you'll notice there's not much room!... "

July 31st 1943 RCW, "usual address" to Home

"This must be very quick in order to catch the person who has so kindly consented to take it to England. I'm well and in the best of

---

[84] Admiral Sir Geoffrey Nigel Oliver: was commander of Force "N" in July 1943, with its HQ at the Algiers naval base HMS *Hannibal*, for Operation Husky, the invasion of Sicily which took place on 9 July. (http://en.wikipedia.org/wiki/Geoffrey_Oliver)

health in spite of the heat and hope you are all the same. If you do not yet know the 'usual address' hang on until my air letter arrives which will give it... "

Aug 7th 1943 CEW to RCW, 126 Flotilla HMS *Hannibal* airletter

"So this is the way to get letters to you i.e. by Air Mail... Anyway we were delighted to have your airmail letter dated July 27th... John still around no call up yet... Yes we saw DB once... One thing from an old hand leave the women alone! At all costs. Don't pile up fearful regrets on the very doorstep of what I pray may be a long, happy and useful career... not preaching – it's an old head talking to a young un... The spring offensive at no 9 *{Holmwood Gdns}* continues with unabated ferocity – the casualties among my wardrobe and personal possessions continue to be frightful... "

Aug 7th 1943 RCW address as above to Home

"I've lost my fountain pen in the sea... so pencil... This is an incredible town [Algiers] and one I've no wish to visit again – everything smells horrible and... very expensive... As a matter of fact I haven't smoked more than 20 since leaving England... I haven't much appetite one doesn't out here... "

Aug 14th 1943 CEW to RCW, 126 Flotilla HMS *Hannibal*

"... Shorter daylight starts tomorrow black out at 8.50 (after about 10) don't like this starting. Visions of knocking into things on way home. Wonder if it's necessary. The news seems to indicate we're moving forward but it's hard to make head or tale of it... "

Aug 28th 1943 CEW to RCW, 126 Flotilla HMS *Hannibal*

"... John... no call up for him yet though all my 18s here have gone already from here... "

Sept 1st 1943 RCW, 126 Flotilla Naval Party 869E c/o GPO (censor) to Home

"I don't suppose you will have heard from me for some time – well the reason is that I've left the last place and am at sea again – such is life but I'm not sorry it's cooler anyway, more comfortable and the food – well it surpasses anything I've ever had! We are kept very busy and I think I'm at least earning my keep – And also some leave!

But when that will be – lord knows!... I have not received any letters from you for some time but that's natural enough with all my moving around... How's John getting on... I think he's being extraordinarily lucky *{re 'call up'}* don't you. If he can hold out much longer I believe the war will be almost over!... "

Sept 5th 1943 JRW to RCW, 126 Flotilla Naval Party 869E c/o GPO

"... a few lines having seen the evening's visitors home, namely JL and P who is home for the weekend... Mummie has apparently cross-examined DB over his 48 hour romance and finds he is swept off his feet completely, also he is thoroughly fed up because he has been sent on a journey abroad... Pat sends her love... "

Sept 12th 1943 JRW, Home to RCW, 126 Flotilla Naval Party 869E c/o GPO

"... On Wednesday evening I was informed I had to go to Port Glasgow the next day with a whole lot of equipment. Well I know what you had said about that journey and believe me I found it all true. As for Port Glasgow (it's about 2 miles from Greenock) well it's better left unwritten. We were working on a picture called 'Out of Chaos' which is about artists in wartime. The artist who we had with us, and who incidentally has several pictures in the National Gallery was completely eccentric. Do you know he hadn't had a bath for seven years and he never washed or brushed his hair. His clothes were absolutely filthy and he always wore his pyjamas under his suit the top half of which acted as a shirt... I was glad to get back from that job... We will put your name down for a fountain pen and then you should have it as soon as you can get home... "

Sept 15th 1943 RCW, 126 Flotilla Naval Party 869E c/o GPO (censor) to Home

"I have only time to tell you that I'm well and safe. I expect that you have and still are listening to the old 'news' – well that will, no doubt, give you all the information at present allowed but I've been in the thick of it! *{probably Salerno landings & Operation Avalanche see*

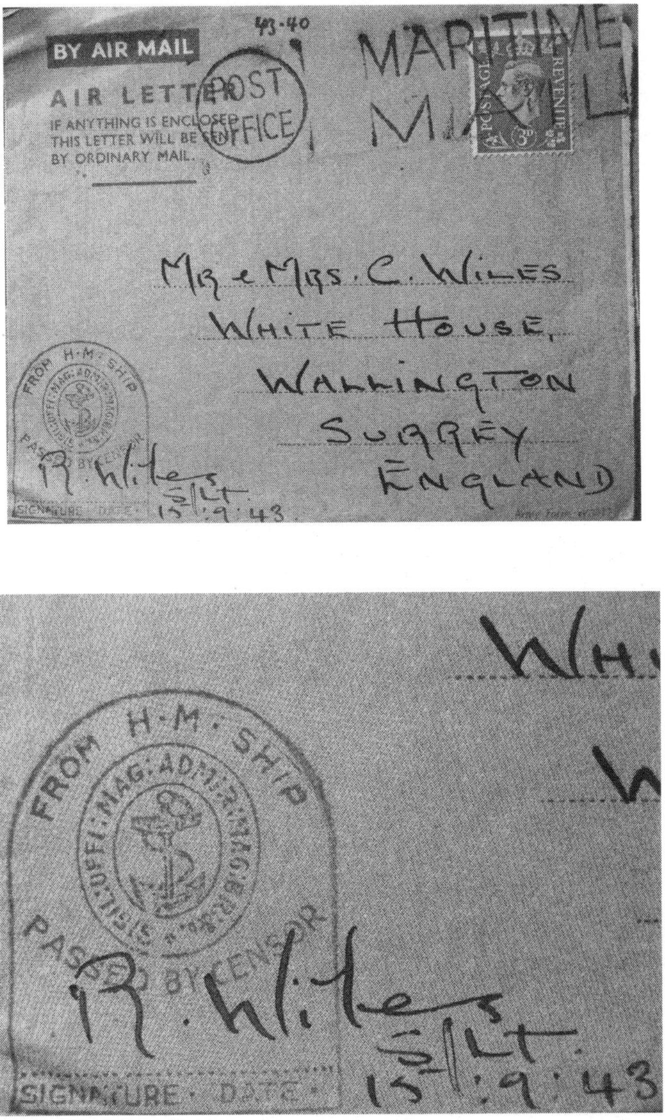

Fig 27 Example of censored mail from active service - RCW as his own censor!

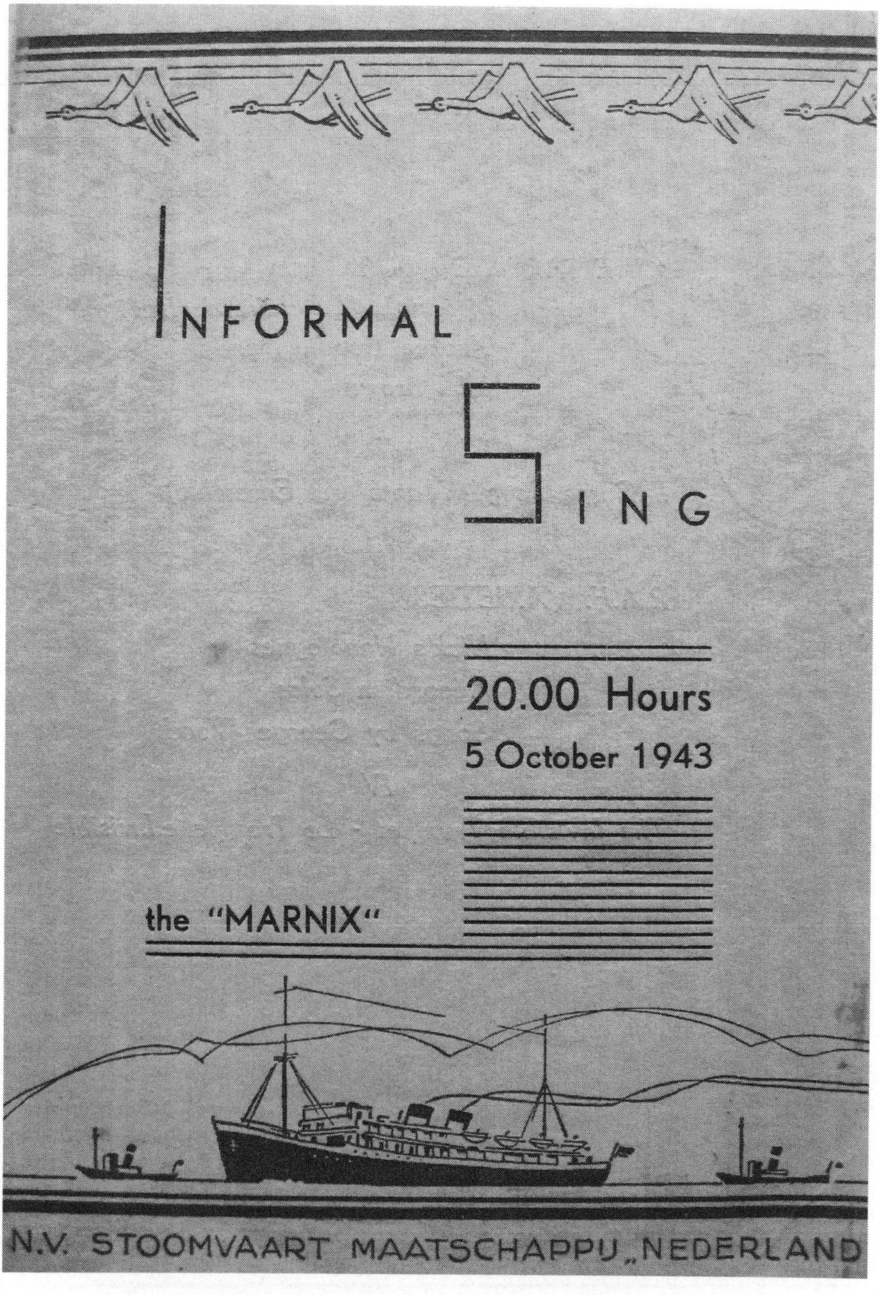

Fig 28 Singsong programme (see opposite for inside)

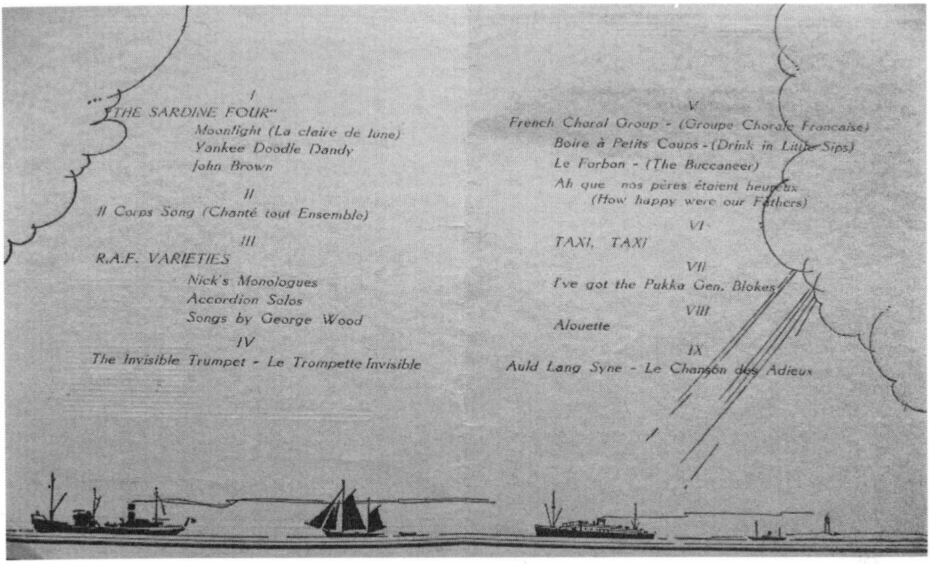

Fig 28 Singsong programme Oct 5th 1943 during return to Algiers on Marnix van sint Aldegonde (see also figs 8/9)

footnote 27 above[85]*}* And thank heavens have been luckier than many. I have received no letters from you, somewhat naturally, but believe some are close at hand so I'm looking forward to getting them... So don't worry hope everybody on 'top line'... "

(one month before ship sunk by German action)

Oct 29th 1943 RCW, 126 Flotilla PO Box 8 Southend to Home

"Nothing fresh to report – life goes on here just the same almost all tedious little office jobs at the moment but very comfortable quarters and good food. I spent nearly all Thursday trying to sort out

---

[85] *Salerno Landings. Operation Avalanche* - the main invasion at Salerno by the U.S. 5th Army - began on 9 September, and in order to secure surprise, the decision had been taken to assault without preliminary naval or aerial bombardment. However, tactical surprise was not achieved, as the naval commanders had predicted. As the first wave of the U.S. 36th Infantry Division approached the shore at Paestum a loudspeaker from the landing area proclaimed in English: *"Come on in and give up. We have you covered."* The Allied troops attacked nonetheless.
Extracts from http://en.wikipedia.org/wiki/Allied_invasion_of_Italy (http://creativecommons.org/licenses/by-sa/3.0/)

flotilla pay queries at head offices but managed to drop into H's *{Harrods}* for lunch and a haircut. W *{godfather}* and his wife were almost at the next table and both came over to speak to me. I also saw Mrs A & T *{family friends}* who is a Sargent Pilot just back from Canada. Incidentally she has moved to a flat in Queen's Gate... Now for a tale of woe!! My suit has arrived from H's and it's truly b...y after all those fittings – the coat looks like a sack and has an almost humorous aspect which of course won't do at all. I don't quite know what to do about it as I am unable to get up to town at any old time and I have only one suit here... Anyway could you let me have my old suit immediately as if I continue wearing my present one all the time I won't have a respectable suit at all. I am very disappointed about the whole business as you can well imagine. Perhaps Daddy could mention it to Mr L when he gets the chance... "

Nov 15th 1943 RCW, 126 Flotilla PO Box 8 Southend to Home

"... We have been up to our eyes in it here with only 2 officers and 135 men to look after and each evening we feel about 'cooked'. I wrote to L about my suit and enclose his reply in the meantime let's hope he credits my account... Thanks a lot M *{OLW}* for all the trouble you must have taken over it – I was more than surprised with the result. I am hoping to be home some-time Friday for the weekend... P*{friend}* tells me that she may possibly get that weekend as well. Daddy mentioned Great Universal in his letter, I wonder, did he see that long article with photos of IW and family in the Express last week – simply astounding but disgraceful that a newspaper should publish a man stating he had spent £30000 on decorating his flat in wartime out of the shareholders' money I should imagine. I don't expect to be here much longer but as long as it's not Scotland again! things won't be so bad. A letter from Dormer *{Lt Dormer see fig 7}* a few days ago says he's returning in 2 weeks time but doesn't know whether he'll take over the flotilla again – I doubt it though. Well cheerio... "

Nov 18th 1943 HMS Copra *{see footnote 30, p26}*: attached as Divisional Officer to 126 Personnel Flotilla vice Warneford.

Dec 1943 ?exact date: RCW (top of letter excised censor *{appears to be RCW again!}* no stamp– at sea) to All, Home

"It was good to hear you on the phone last night… As I told you I shall not be home for the 25th but we are due for 10 days or so in a month's time… I am writing this in my cabin which is rather small – of the warship variety as opposed to the last one I had – nevertheless it's warm and very comfortable which is what matters in this climate!… "

Dec 5th 1943 RCW 552 Flotilla HMS *Foliot 1,* Tormentor… Plymouth *{censor himself}* to Home

"… Doubtless the absence of a stamp on this letter will explain many things even if the address doesn't. But don't worry. I think the offer of £424 for the car a really magnificent one and Daddy certainly shouldn't fail to take it… Incidentally I saw in Dec 3rd Country Life a house recommended by H's – Choicest Part of Purley *{CEW & OLW actually moved to Purley in 1952}*… might be worth having a look at. Naturally I am unable to say much as I have to censor this myself! But it's hard work and plenty of it. I am almost certain that I should be home for Christmas but one never knows… "

Dec 25th 1943 RCW HMS *Ceres* c/o GPO to All, Home

"Christmas morning and where am I!!!? Anyway I'm quite used to it by now so I don't really mind. Thank you all Daddy and Mummie for your letters and presents – incidentally my present for M *{OLW}* is ordered but not to hand yet. I have received quite a number of cards as well – which all go to decorate my cabin. The enclosed letter was written I should imagine by Lady W… together with a cheque for £5… extraordinarily good of them to remember me at a time like this…" (2nd page missing)

1944

Jan 14th 1944 RCW, Home on leave (CEW diary)

Feb 2nd 1944 RCW, HMS *Foliot*, Tormentor Foliot, Plymouth to Home

"... I have never before seen so much countryside under water as there was on the way! Here things about as bad as the last spot - bad living conditions and so far ceaseless wind and rain!... "

April 15th 1944 RCW, 552 LCA *{Landing Craft Assault}* Flotilla c/o GPO to Home

"... Thank you both for your thoughts and wishes of last Sunday and for the most welcome enclosures... It hardly seemed like a birthday at all as we were on the go most of the time and in any case the atmosphere wasn't quite the same as a year ago! The sweets were consumed with great rapidity one evening in my cabin by 4 of us – didn't last so very long as you can imagine but they were enjoyed!... I'm trying to send some laundry home – I've simply masses of it and no possible chance of getting any done... no other news not even a trip to the cinema... "

May 5th 1944 RCW, Glasgow Telegram to Home

"all well writing Dick"

May 8th 1944 FM, *{RCW billeted with family}* Plymouth to RCW 552 Flotilla c/o GPO

"... so kind of you to thank me for having had you here. It was a great pleasure... I heard from E *{FM's son}* the other day and he was able by putting "small" to let me know he is in that type of L.C. *{Landing Craft}* evidently like yours. I am grateful to you for describing them. I feel I know a little about them now. J [86] does not like being confined to "darkest Sheerness" as she puts it. Don't forget to let us know what you are doing and where - we are interested & wish you well... "

May 20th 1944 RCW to OLW (unheaded/unaddressed paper)

"Dear Mummie, Enclosed laundry as promised also my best boots

---

[86] J (FM's daughter) wrote to CMW after RCW died in 1994 indicating how fond she had been of him: he gave her a gold disc & chain for her 21st with a naval crown on one side and "J.... from Dick" on the other.

(just look at them!). Please have same repaired and (right boot) needs stitching here! *{diagram}* then keep them at home. Hope you enjoy the enclosed sweets. Love Dick PS Retain all this laundry unless I wire for it please. Excuse scrawl D."

May 26th 1944 RCW, 552 LCA Flotilla, c/o GPO (opened by censor) to Home

"Thank you for being so prompt with my laundry which reached me a few days ago, quite intact! I hope that the tin of sweets has reached you in a similar condition... Well I'm afraid there's no news – that is news I can tell you, there's plenty that I can't as you may well guess."

June 14th 1944 CEW, Home to JRW

"Hello Boy: This is the so-called News and this is Dad writing it – and let's get cracking: First, thanks for yours from 'Diomede'[87] (how DO you pronounce it?) which is just to hand. "Calm before the storm"... you didn't mention 'calm' before that I remember! Perhaps it only seems like calm, looking backwards! Anyway you did get a sleep to start with... that – phone again!... Lieutenant Reed enquiring what news of Dick. Glad to be able to tell him – and you – that he rang through the day after D-day about 10pm –"just to let you know I'm all right: I thought you'd like to hear"! Beyond that the Admiral *{RCW}* wasn't to be drawn... he'd tell us when he got home. When? "Couldn't possibly say". Anyway he sounded cheerful enough, even if I thought there was "just a suspicion (as Basil *{CEW's brother}* says) of 'heavy doings' behind his very guarded phrasing. Since then, silence, and I trust he's still fine and hearty – but I can't regard it at all as 'Monty' does – "a terrific party" – indeed – 'terrific' – indeed, but 'party' – no! M *{Mick - nickname for OLW}* was presented with a certificate somewhere last night by the Civil Defence Workers... for her help. It was all lettered in 'Old English' by a too obvious amateur but the kindly thought was there and M lugged it home, oak frame and all, as proudly as if it were an Old Master!... My own contribution to Sea Power (as chairman of cadets) is not yet recognised even by C... and the last meeting nearly 'broke up in disorder'. He's

[87] HMS Diomede served as a training ship from 1943-45. (http://www.battleships-cruisers.co.uk/d_class.htm#HMS%20Diomede)

impossible and my impressive Naval experience couldn't work up a salvo to silence him!... We're 'Saluting the Soldier'[88] this week with a few well-meaning Flags and Streamers and a shocking model of 'Lil ole Itler' at Wallington Station who gobbles pennies and lifts his arm or something – a shocking affair. M in the thick of it couldn't give me the faintest idea of progress or comparison with last year... "

July 23rd 1944 RCW, 552 LCA Flotilla c/o GPO to Home

"I'm still alive and well although by now you're doubtless beginning to think otherwise... great deal of work and as a result - no leave... It's nearly 7 months since I had 7 days you know... I'm glad to hear that the White House *{Home in Wallington}* has survived to date but I can well believe from all accounts that these things are exceedingly unpleasant... J's Auntie *{see footnote 86}* has lent me a portable gramophone and we've managed to get some records together – so life on board has brightened a little... "

July 23rd 1944 RCW, 552 LCA Flotilla c/o GPO to JRW address as above

"... I haven't had any [leave] for 7 months... on the move all the time since 'D' day. There's a great deal I could tell you, but of course it can't be written... I ran into DB - first time in two years - went aboard his ship for dinner and talked... mostly girls! He hasn't altered a bit. They seem to be getting a very unpleasant time at home – safer at sea I think!... "

Sept 5th 1944 CEW to RCW 552 LCA Flotilla c/o GPO

"... The weather today is shocking but the Doodle-bugs haven't been these last three days - thank heaven – and I'm hopeful we've seen the last of 'em... nevertheless I fear he'll find something pretty bad to hand out before he's done... We must review sleeping upstairs again but so far we're in the cellar still... "

---

[88] 'Salute the Soldier' Week was a scheme to encourage people to save their money in Government accounts, such as War Bonds, Savings Bonds, Defence Bonds and Savings Certificates. (http://www.brandonatwar.co.uk/salute_the_soldier.htm)

Sept 9th 1944 DB, HMS *Wren* to RCW addressed to home

"... No doubt you heard about my last ship and here I am again, once more at sea. Still I did manage nearly five weeks leave... the wife and I... in the Lake District... Grasmere. This is a very different proposition from the last ship and really I couldn't have wished for a better job. I'm no. 1 here & have a grand crowd of officers... I didn't go south of Liverpool during my leave mainly because of the doodlebugs... I suppose you are still keeping the old heart locked away until after the war. Well old boy you won't have to wait long now. The news certainly is on the up & up... "

Sept 12th 1944 RCW, 552 LCA Flotilla to OLW/CEW and separate to JRW

"... It's very relieving to hear about the bombs although I hope everyone isn't rushing back to London too soon! What price the blackout as well! Isn't Daddy pleased? I must say things have certainly taken on a different aspect even since I was on leave... DK *{PK's sister}* is being married on 23rd Sept... Managed to see 'For Whom the Bell Tolls'... it's terrific. I still get occasional letter from Pat... "

Sept 17th 1944 CEW to RCW, 552 LCA Flotilla c/o GPO

"... The 'P... lady' walked in yesterday... 7pm with a blonde contraption for company and giggled part of eternity away until midnight - I suppose they were invited - whether they were or not I see neither point nor wisdom in it - 'consideration' I have long ceased to look for. The best I can say is that the blonde affair struck me as being the less empty of the two. Boy, beware of EMPTINESS!... a bomb cracked behind me on the way [from the office] and shook me... Still a few bombs daily, and nightly, one at 6 o.c. this morning: sometimes an alert, sometimes no sound till the crash, happily not in the district so far: would seem pick-a-backs and rockets but no one seems to know... But it's a mellow morning – peace – a sky of sapphire without a cloud – and lovely sunshine – God be thanked... "

Sept 25th 1944 RCW telegram to Home

"Parcel of laundry in post please retain do not write until you hear from me Dick"

Oct 1st 1944 RCW, 552 LCA Flotilla, c/o GPO to Home

"So glad to have heard you again last night and learn that all is well on the Home Front… I don't believe I told you before but Lieut P [89] has left and I have a new 'boss' called 'Dobson'. Born & lived in Wallington for about 18 years, isn't it extraordinary? Anyway he's a likeable type and seems to know the job. Lt P has at last got his leave to go home – Jamaica. As you know he has been 8 years away… Will you please send on one pair of pyjamas, some socks, underwear and 2 or 3 shirts – no more for the time being. The address is as usual… "

Oct 23rd 1944 RCW, 552 LCA Flotilla, c/o GPO to Home (Censor) in pencil

"Just to tell you that I'm safe and well on the Continent! Plenty of fruit and everyone very glad to see us, especially the children if we have any chocolate or sweets – some haven't seen any for a long, long time! Living is very rough and would like to be home now! Have already seen a great many places I don't suppose either of you have. But you'll have to wait for my homecoming before I can give any names. Hope you are all well, don't worry. All my love Dick. PS Please pass this on to John"

Nov 1st 1944 RCW to Home (stamped Field Post Office, passed by Censor)

"I am quite well. *{printed}* I will send you a letter as soon as possible. I have received no letter from you lately *{all printed}* R Wiles *{signed}" {See fig 29 below & page 35 – Oct 29th 1944}*

[89] See letters Nov 18th 1944 & April 14th 1945 below

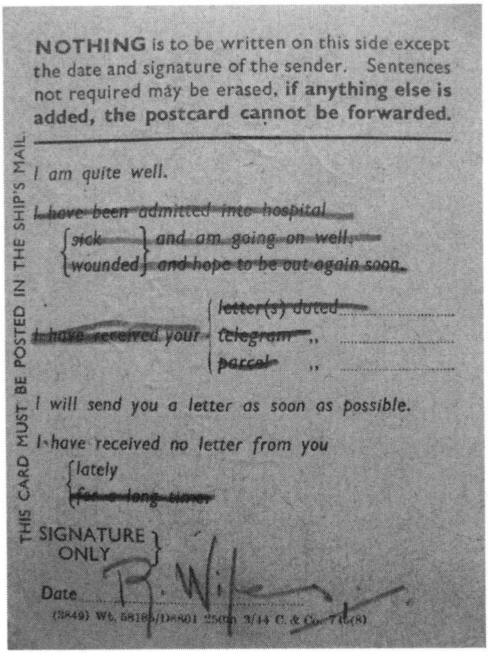

THIS CARD MUST BE POSTED IN THE SHIP'S MAIL.

NOTHING is to be written on this side except the date and signature of the sender. Sentences not required may be erased. **If anything else is added, the postcard cannot be forwarded.**

I am quite well.

~~*I have been admitted into hospital*~~

~~*sick*~~ ~~*and am going on well.*~~
~~*wounded*~~ ~~*and hope to be out again soon.*~~

~~*I have received your*~~ ~~*letter(s) dated*~~ ....
~~*telegram*~~ ,, ...
~~*parcel*~~ ,, ...

I will send you a letter as soon as possible.

I have received no letter from you
lately
~~*for a long time.*~~

SIGNATURE ONLY } B. Wi...

Date ....

(3849) Wt. 58186/D8801 250m 3/44 C. & Co. 716(8)

Fig 29 Official notification of 'problem' sent to CEW/OLW at home

Nov 2nd 1944 RCW, 12th Canadian General Hospital, Canadian Army Overseas B.W.E.F to Home

"Dear All, In spite of the above I'm fairly well and still intact. Doubtless you have put two and two together over the recent news and more or less guessed of my activities and whereabouts I ran into a spot of bother but nothing serious so here I am – extremely comfortable and well looked after. Please don't bother to write to this address as I may be moved – anyway I'll keep you posted. Excuse this dreadful scrawl but I'm in bed on my back – not exactly ideal! Cheerio for now – don't worry – All love Dick"

Nov 5th 1944 AM, 24th Canadian General Hospital, Somewhere in England (sic) (1st Bn Regina Rifle Regt, c/o I C I R U Canadian Army England) to CEW/OLW, Home

"Dear Sir or Madam: Arriving back to this country I asked a Red Cross Officer to phone you this message: 'I was in hospital somewhere in

Belgium where I met you (sic) son S/Lt R.C. Wiles. He is in the best condition except that sore in the back. When I left him, xray were taken and no fracture noted'. You will certainly received a word from him soon telling you how everything happened; but there is no use to worry. His hospitalisation can be called a 'very well earned rest'. Will he be lucky enough to come back to U.K. and spend Xmas with you, I don't know. Doctors never teach a word of our destiny in our presence. But I hope so, it will be grand for all of you to be together again. I told him that if I was coming over here to do my best to let you know. Unfortunately I cannot get up and phone you but the Red Cross Officer did it for me. I must close now this letter full of mistakes, I'm still a student of your language. At home I always speak French. Hoping to hear soon of R.C. I'm closing now. Respectfully yours. AM"

Nov 5th 1944 JRW, Royal Naval College, Greenwich SE10 to RCW, 552 LCA Flotilla c/o GPO

"I was on the 'phone home this morning and I hear from Mummie that you are in hospital or something – all very vague. It's damn bad luck and I hope its nothing much... I hope to go on leave at the end of this week and if I do I intend spending a day or two down in Bristol. Who knows what may happen after that? Things aren't as quiet as they might be around here – V-2s etc but we might be the hell of a lot worse off; I have no doubt it's considerably more peaceful than where you have been... "

Nov 7th 1944 RCW (Hospital, Belgium) to JRW, Royal Naval College, Greenwich forwarded to Home (Censor)

"Was ever so pleased to get your letter, the first I've had in nearly 4 weeks! I've no doubt that your shrewd guess as to my activities is quite correct and will be made even more definite by the fact I'm in hospital. There's nothing to worry over though. This is a Canadian Army Hospital and I'm treated really well and should at least be out of bed in another 3 or 4 days. You're lucky to have 'made' Greenwich – yes I know all about the terrific food! A rather different story to that over here! – However the fruit situation is almost unbelievable – unlimited quantities of almost every kind E.G. Grapes 1/- per pound!!! (Harrods price 25/-)! Fancy N *{family friend}* getting married, what's the fellow like – sheer lunacy! as Daddy would say... I'm afraid that I'm unable to say when I shall get leave but somehow I don't think that it will be so very long... PS Excuse the writing am on my back"

Nov 18th 1944 Lt C.Pratt (see p31) Tighnabruaich, Argyllshire to RCW 552 Flotilla GPO London

"Many thanks for your last letter received whilst at Northney[90]... Unfortunately I cannot quite make out who has done each individual landing. I noticed "991" at Walcheren, but unfortunately it was one of those turned over to ---(sic). We completed our 3 weeks here and then went on 8 days leave before returning again for N^y^... If you or E... or anyone else feel you want to continue I Minors I suggest putting in for N^y^ now – It will mean quite a lot of leave before L.SI *{Landing Ship Infantry}* & then Far East!! If you want to share one ask Q. to hold you over until I return in February. It would mean doing the first part up here about the Middle of December... "

Nov 19th 1944 A.S, HMS *Lulworth* c/o British Fleet Mail to RCW (censored)

"... you'll remember that odd type who used to see quite a lot of you at K.A.*{King Alfred}*. How's life treating you these days?... I suppose you've had one or two excitements; were you in the invasion? I've been in this ship the whole time & in the Indian Ocean for the last year, so have missed all the great doings nearer home. Those carefree days at K.A. seem very far away, & I'm afraid I'm now looking forward to the day when I become a civilian once again. No one will find me joining the Navy for good; I rather imagine those are your feelings too. I've had practically no excitements, not that I'm eager for any, & have had 2 gorgeous leaves about which I could write a book but unfortunately censorship won't let me say where I spent them. The seas are pleasantly calm in this part of the world which is a relief for the stomach; I never did like the Atlantic... life might be a lot worse. What are you going to do after the war? There seems to be very little time to think about it these days, especially as

---

[90] HMS *Northney*, HMS Northney I, HMS Northney II, HMS Northney III and HMS Northney IV] Hayling Island, England landing craft training base http://en.wikipedia.org/wiki/List_of_Royal_Navy_shore_establishments

demobilisation is bound to take a long time. It's difficult to know what jobs there will be going too; I want to go up to Cambridge if there's a chance [91]... "

Dec 7th 1944 Uncle Ted *{married to Terese – OLW's sister}*, Richmond Hill Bristol to JRW (HMS *Lochinvar*[92])

"... We missed you very much when you had gone... and then just as we are getting used to routine life again – straight from the blue Dick arrives, while we were thinking he was being nicely tucked up by a good looking nurse in Belgium. We had a nice time together – did the same things as you did – coffee – flicks – Empire Music Hall & jaw until it was time to go to bed. Of course we heard all about the latest addition to Dicks list of "sweethearts" – we shall have to wait to see how long the latest attack will last... I am busy at the Manpower Board and Auntie is very industrious making dolls clothes and a really wonderful doll for the Red X Fund at the office – as Dick would say 'It's a smasher and will really shake them'... Grandma *{OLW and Terese's mother}* is reading all the newspapers... Ted"

Dec 31st 1944 CEW to RCW ?where

"... God bless you boy and again Peace in 1945"

---

[91] AS subsequently went up to Cambridge, where he studied agriculture.

[92] HMS *Lochinvar* was a minesweeping training "stone frigate" (shore establishment) of the Royal Navy, sited at Port Edgar on the Firth of Forth in Scotland. http://en.wikipedia.org/wiki/HMS_Lochinvar_(shore_establishment)

1945

Jan 9th 1945 RCW, 552 Flotilla to JRW, Home

"... No doubt you will be joining a ship shortly – let me know her name and keep a look out for old K. Life for me is utterly boring... don't think I've ever before been quite so fed up except of course at D.Hs *{DH Evans}*! Fortunately... receiving fairly frequent communications from Brugge which are at least keeping me alive... "

Fig 30 – see legend next page

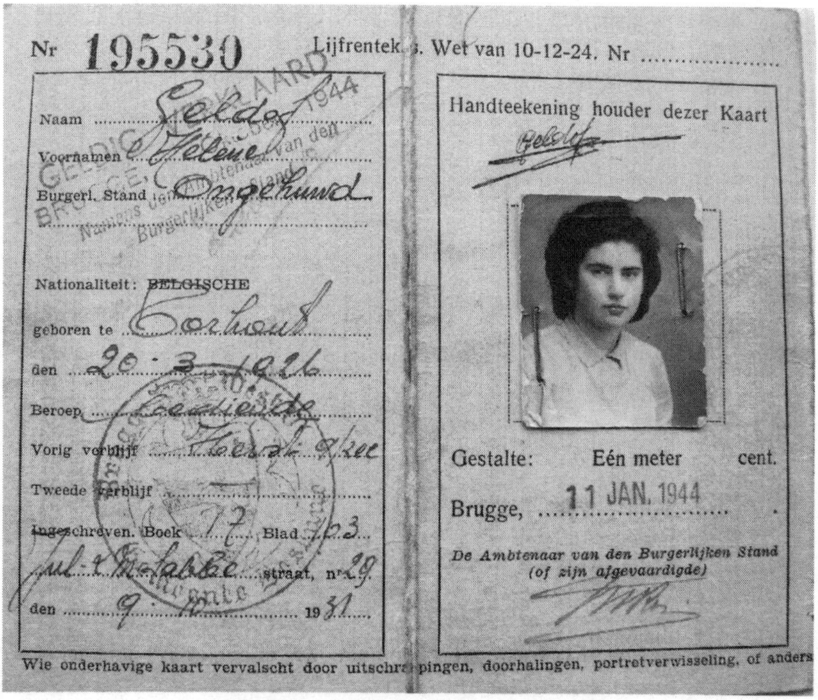

Nr 195530 Lijfrentek. 3. Wet van 10-12-24. Nr ....

Naam Geldof

Voornamen Hélène

Burgerl. Stand Ongehuwd

Nationaliteit: BELGISCHE

geboren te Torhout

den 20 · 3 · 1926

Beroep ....

Vorig verblijf ....

Tweede verblijf ....

Ingeschreven. Boek 17 Blad 123

.... straat, nr 29

den 9 1931

Handteekening houder dezer Kaart

Geldof

Gestalte: Eén meter cent.

Brugge, 11 JAN. 1944 .

De Ambtenaar van den Burgerlijken Stand (of zijn afgevaardigde)

Wie onderhavige kaart vervalscht door uitschrappingen, doorhalingen, portretverwisseling, of anders

Fig 30 The source of "frequent communications from Brugge" Hélène Geldof (see letter above) – age 17 at time of photo.

Jan 14th 1945 CEW, Home to RCW, LCA 552 Flotilla

"… Glad to hear of your 'war increment' (that's what 'M' *{OLW}* says it is). She has bought your *{savings}* certificates and pasted them in your book. Carry on the good work – you'll need all the 'nest eggs' you can muster in this brave-new-busted-world-to-be… It has been a week of fog, thick snow, ice, then indecipherable slush, trains bunged up, stations chaotic, arrivals hours late, wet feet, frozen limbs… And plenty of V1s and V2s chucked in – though happily not too near. Bad one near Peter Jones and the Pensioner's Hospital (think hit). One on the line somewhere and staff arrived at 12 o.c. next day… Special exhibition of paintings by Mervyn Peake & wife at Peter Jones… "

Jan 21st 1945 CEW, Home to RCW, LCA 552 flotilla

"… world - as I write that last word a V2 somewhere in the offing… M *{OLW}* making marmalade: she says it's marmalade! M sent your cigarettes off (for a Duke) *{Balkan Sobranie}* why not Weights?... Whether you are on sea or land I hope you'll keep well and smiling and that a kindly Providence who has watched over us all so far will bless you and keep you from all harm. Almost looks at long last as if the dreadful night is ending!... "

Jan 21st 1945 RCW, 552 LCA Flotilla to Home

"Sorry my phone call was so vague the other evening but you know how things are and the care one must exercise. However I've no doubt that you managed to gather that I was off on my travels once again! So don't worry if my letters become somewhat more spaced out... I enjoyed D's *{Daddy's}* letter very much... PS Tell M not to forget to wear the glasses when she gets them."

Jan 28th 1945 RCW, 552 LCA Flotilla to Home (censor)

"Here's to let you know that I'm over in Belgium once again – terribly cold. But well protected with fur-lined coats and gloves!... I have been extremely fortunate in having been able to see Hélène two or three times – all of which has given me added fortification to face the tasks ahead. The outlook seems to be growing brighter daily and I think the end is not so far away, at any rate in this theatre of war. Of course none of us has received any mail as yet but doubtless it will catch us up... Well the ink's running out of my pen – so must finish... P.S. I believe H *{Hélène}* may send Mummie a card – don't be surprised... "

Feb 1st 1945 A *{naval friend}*, GPO Box No 8, Southend on Sea to RCW 552 LCA Flotilla c/o Force 'T'

"I've wondered where the will of Pugsley *{see pages 37/38 re Captain Pugsley}* and CO have taken you. I anxiously watch the newspapers and hope to see startling headlines. You will see the draft eventually came. JE and myself to old Westcliff ?*punching our course out at* Jimmy Cook. Fortunately I have only another day here... N is D.O. *{Divisional Officer}* of 550 and two officers have taken our place, sent for operational experience so say the authorities... I feel singularly fortunate in seeing the last of Cricket *{p32}*. Like you I haven't a good word for the place and as you... foresaw, exercises are in full swing. Very curious to know if you have managed to see Hélène. I hope this interest of your life is, as you would wish yourself. Remember I want to be in at the Wedding... My regards to Lt Dobson, Dick Roger, Cooper & Max. It was a damned shame about Farmer. Off now to bed. Good hunting, A... "

Fig 31 RCW & Hélène Geldof at Ostend docks Aug 23rd 1945

Feb 4th 1945 CEW, Home to RCW, 552 LCA Flotilla

" The ink has run out of your pen this time, has it? Bless my soul. But never mind it's well to know you're fit and happy though I refrain from comment on the feminine fortification – all I would say there is would it endure all down the stormy highway which is Life? And what of her stock – and family history – apt to be brushed aside but so frightfully vital... Spent some time yesterday with the Most Noble the

Earl of E... – whose forbear gave Drake his orders at the Armada – oh dear oh dear – the Aristocracy of England – certainly he'll never give any such orders, and no one would listen if he did!... Still I suppose Adolph is thinking he's got worse troubles... Yesterday afternoon Cavalry Club with F. discussing the Harrods Book.[93] Superb hospitality, after 3 hours of hard going – one cup of tea –not a biscuit... "

Feb 4th 1945 RCW, 552 LCA Flotilla Naval Party 1740x c/o BFMO Reading to Home

"... All I may tell you is that I am now in Holland and kept fairly busy... some of the days and nights I've spent over here have been quite the coldest I've ever experienced!!... As Daddy says 'it looks as if the night is ending' – they're being 'pasted' properly now – wonder how Hitler feels about it all – in 12 years exactly from nothing to the most powerful man in the world and right down again! –it's quite incredible... We manage to get an occasional film and ENSA[94] show to brighten a 'dull' life up. Believe me England's a wonderful spot after... these foreign places!... don't worry and note new address... "

Feb 9th 1945 Naval Message FROM NC FORCE T TO RNO BEVELAND R NOYC ANTWERP FORCE T GOES FO 509 & 552

"Request you will sail 16 LCA of 509 and 552 Flotillas from Hansweert {*south side of Zeeland west of Antwerp*} to Antwerp at 0800 tomorrow Friday"

Feb 10th 1945 CEW, (office Sat pm 3.30) to RCW ?where

"... John is home on leave... off he went forthwith and squandered his substance on 'tropical kit' – doesn't yet know when he'll have to go half across the world... he seems to have visions of taking Hollywood in his stride – perhaps... "

Feb 15th 1945 RCW, c/o 90th Field Company, Royal Engineers B.L.A. to

---

93 Book about the history of Harrods by F. though uncertain if published

94 The Entertainments National Service Association , or ENSA *{apocryphally 'Every Night Something Awful'}* was set up in 1939 by Basil Dean and Leslie Henson to provide entertainment for British armed forces personnel during World War II. ENSA operated as part of the Navy, Army and Air Force Institutes. (http://en.wikipedia.org/wiki/Entertainments_National_Service_Association)

OLW

"... my new address... no I'm not in the army though it may appear so... In good health and spirits but unfortunately without any mail... Can't say where I am naturally but it's well into things!!... Have you received your glasses yet? – if so, don't forget to wear 'em! And in any case don't go overdoing things... don't worry... "

Feb 18th 1945 CEW, (office Sat 2pm) to RCW, 552 LCA Flotilla, Naval party 1740X, c/o BFMO Reading

"... John is still with us... one or two nights out with the film person (don't know her name), trips to town and to Merton Park etc. He's very fit and looks forward to seeing Sydney... Not so many V2s this week but perhaps they're going elsewhere. What an appalling business it all is – now this Japan affair. As you say it MUST be nearing its end, but even if it is what WILL be the state of Europe and the world! All broke and busted... I think M is getting used to her glasses – she was actually reading a book last night!"

Feb 22nd 1945 Mlle VB, Rennes, France to RCW, Home

"My dear Dick... We have received a postcard from Miss G. *{Headmistress St Hildas, where JRW & RCW went to primary school, VB was there before the war started but returned home to France}* I am very proud for you because you are in the Royal Navy and your brother. My brother is voluntary for the war, he is in the... army, he fighting in Alsace and he will wounded but not too bad... We have not been so miserable for the food, in Brittany we are rich in butter, eggs, apples but the germans taking really all but I have been many times to the country with my bicycle to get a little in the farm. I work in a office for the insurance social... always busy... I can speak English at home because we have a English soldier RAF who come every week he leave at Reading and when he come I am spoilt. I hope you are not jealous you must not. Give my regards to your parents... " (sic)

Feb 23rd 1945 JRW, Home to RCW, 90th Field Company Royal Engineers B.L.A.

"We were delighted to get your letter dated Feb 15th... it was almost a fortnight since we heard... and were wondering how you were getting on... am expecting to move off very soon. There's no need to tell you where I am going, I am just following the rest of the navy. It's a long way but there you are, can't be helped... "

Feb 25th 1945 CEW, Home to RCW ?where

"Yours of 15th was mighty welcome – but can't understand your not getting mine – I've written you a long one every week without missing – surely they'll come to hand... P... inviting herself as usual. Phone rings again MP... inviting herself... What is this place? – Home for Incurable Intruders – that's all... John and I to a prize fight at Penge yesterday – the sea cadets qualifying bouts – for the final at Albert hall. Boy what you missed!... "

Mar 2nd 1945 RCW, 90th Field Company, Royal Engineers, B.L.A. to Home

"You will be pleased to learn that all your letters have now reached me. Even the one D posted to me last Dec containing the photos... Thanks for the enclosed article from the Mail *{?sent CEW 25th Feb}* as a matter of fact... it was a subject of lengthy discussion in the mess!..." 2nd page missing

Mar 3rd 1945 CEW, Home to RCW, 90th Field Company, Royal Engineers

"... More sirens – more bombs – getting ugly... "

Mar 6th 1945 Abdulla & Co Ltd, 112 Commercial St E.1. to RCW 552 LCA Flotilla c/o GPO London

Invoice for "300 Abdulla No 11: 18s 9d"

Mar 10th 1945 CEW to RCW, 90th Field Company, Royal Engineers

"Out of the blue, as it were, every now and then comes your cheerful assurance that all goes well with you and we are mighty glad to get it... The news of the week is of course that John has set out upon his long long journey *{to Australia}* – his flag flying (well more or less) a certain grim resignation perhaps behind a striving smile. Friday morning he went - leaving an odd ache and emptiness - which none spoke of and which all tried not to show. The 'Glories of War' are hard to appreciate - as much by those who leave us as by those they leave behind... "

Mar 14th 1945 JRW, HMS Golden Hind c/o GPO to RCW

"Well you'll know by now that… I am back to business… "

Mar 15th 1945 RCW, 552 LCA Flotilla Naval Party 1768 c/o BFMO to Home

"… Don't worry about the overdraft I haven't drawn any pay for over 2 months – so I'm still solvent… I have done quite a lot of driving recently in a German car we acquired! In fact when I get my leave, if you are agreeable, I will apply for the foreign service petrol ration to which I am entitled and out with the car!!… I enclose a little snap of Hélène – please return it after perusal!! I'm kept pretty busy in fact if you watch the papers and put 2&2 together you might glean something – anyway I shall be glad when it's the return passage – seems ages since Xmas!… " *{Flotilla at Nijmegen}*

Mar 15th 1945 RCW, (as above, censor) to OLW, Town Hall, Wallington

"Dear M, Did you receive Hélène's P.C. all right… she was worried she had said the wrong thing!! I believe you may <u>only</u> write a P.C."

Mar 18th 1945 CEW, Wallington to RCW ?where

"Coming up from a quiet stroll in the sunshine – no one about – trying to 'sort out' a rather harassed mind – 'lo and behold' (as "ITMA"*{It's That Man Again}* says) a café… has started up by Wallington Green opposite the Pub… Two big hand-lettered bills in what once were windows 'DOODLE BUG TEAS' 'PICK-A-BACK SANDWICHES'… M *{OLW}* tearing to Northampton – back the night following – connected with Home Guards… From John of course so far silence. No news – as in your case – is, pray God, good news. And the sun shines as I write, and the pink blossom across the road heeds neither the wisdom nor the lunacy of man, save only to lift his heart beyond the mud and scum of things, and birds unseen are chorusing to the blue sky and lightly drifting wisps of cloud, and but for an odd boom, a far away engine, the press and the radio, the old world might have come once more to love and sanity and grace. Which, as Euclid might have said, is too absurd… "

Mar 18th 1945 RCW, 552 LCA Flotilla, c/o BFMO Reading to OLW

"I am forwarding this little parcel, the contents of which were made by Hélène... "

Mar 23rd 1945 CEW, Office Sat 2pm to RCW

"I enclose as promised the 'Vecchi'[95] menu card... I wrote the stuff on the front and inside but beyond that am not responsible. As for Epstein's Bust – I ask you: still I understand the place was packed to suffocation... Do you remember W of De La Rue's? His boy John went to Charterhouse. When I looked in on W... at his office his John had just turned up an hour before, in battledress it looked like, from the Far East I understood, for the first visit in 5 years. W handed me 2 packs of Playing Cards – special issue – with pictures of Dunkirk on the back – saying he felt sure you would like to have them. Very kind – but I'll keep 'em for you... Bit more freedom (round us) from V2s... Word from John arrived this week – well about 3 words to be precise 'Have got going – John' and even his date at the top of the paper cut out neatly by the censor... "

Mar 25th 1945 OLW, Home to RCW

"... Have stolen a sheet of your gorgeous large yellow note-paper & envelope to write to Hélène and the letter is all ready to be posted... (Post Office said one could send letter)... he (John) left us on March 9th & all we have received is about 4 lines with the date cut out to say he is on the way... it's an awful thought 2 years at least but one can only work & hope on!! I telephoned S's mother *{family friend}* this morning as I guess she would be worried in the light of the news and we had a good long conversation. She said she was quite well so you can tell S *{with RCW}*. I have seen that boy F about a good deal lately am wondering if he's out for good. Also the senior H was home after 4 years absence & he did not seem much changed except older. And the Paratrooper was home too part of the time. My goodness as we listened to the news yesterday we thought of you all and wondered what you were doing... PS the snap of Hélène is charming."

---

[95] Joseph Vecchi was manager of the Hungaria. He was attending a party to mark 25 years serving the cause of "London's good living". Mrs A.V. Alexander presented him with a bronze bust by Epstein (Evening Standard cutting March 1945)

Mar 29th 1945 RCW, 552 LCA Flotilla, Naval Party 1768, c/o BFMO to Home

"... I am listening to the news, at the same moment as writing – isn't it really great! - nearing the end without a doubt! Everyone feels the same – what say you?... I ran into two fellows from school last week ... "

Apr 2nd 1945 OLW, Home to RCW, 552 LCA Flotilla

"Here's to wish you everything that is good on April 9th... Am hoping these few sweets will reach you... No more news of John... "

Fig 32 LCAs including 'my own boat' at 'Granes Lock' (top), on the Rhine (middle) probably March/April 1945

Apr 10th 1945 RCW, 552 LCA Flotilla c/o FMO to Home

"... I'm afraid there was hardly time to think that I was 23!!! And there was no celebration of any kind nevertheless your wishes and thoughts were more than welcome... By the way which F *{friend from home)* is home – has he been wounded?... There's no need for Dad to worry over my driving any longer, I believe I told you we have 'acquired' an OPEL Super Six (German of course!) and by now I have done a considerable amount of driving!... including some very interesting trips into Germany (talk about England being knocked about – well I leave the rest to your imagination). Am glad to read that the V1 and V2 attacks seem to be dying off – let's hope that state of affairs continues. I simply cannot see how it can go on much longer though... what are Wallington's plans for 'V' night?!!... "

Apr 14th 1945 CEW (office) to RCW

"John there! Wire last Wednesday (April 11) 'Safe, well, love John' marked 'Australia'... Spring cleaning... M *{OLW}* in battledress... the woodworms... War has been pretty near the home-front but never so awful as this. I surrendered pronto – unconditionally – long ago – to the woodworms!... "

Apr 14th 1945 RCW, 552 LCA Flotilla, Naval Party 1768, c/o BFMO to Home (censor)

"A note to let you know everything well with me – if you've been listening to the wireless & reading the papers no doubt you have put

2 & 2 together.[96] No more time just now – except watch the Evening Standard… "

Apr 14th 1945 CP, Tignabruaich to RCW, Home

"Dear Wiles, … I saw a list with your name on for this course but imagine "Europe" has kept you more occupied. Let me know all the dope on 552 as far as censorship will allow… after my Leave *{in Jamaica}*… returned here to work; fortunately I am held as an F.O. *{Flotilla Officer}* and as there are only three life is fairly pleasant. The other F.O.s are getting their half-rings *{probably means promotion to Lt Commander}*, a thing which I have to wait for until much older. No more officers are being taken on so am afraid I cannot help you at the moment. Met A outside COHQ in Feb… also R and F… all turned down don't know why. D (553 flotilla) is here, the remainder are chiefly from the Belgian etc White Ensign Ships… Alex said you had fallen (again) for a lovely young Belgian girl!… "

Apr 15th 1945 S/Lt JRW, R.N.B. Sydney to RCW 552 LCA Flotilla, Naval Party 1768, BFMO Reading

"… haven't yet got my ship… Really you would hardly know there was a war on except for a few uniforms floating about. As for cars, well its just amazing for although petrol is rationed there are simply hundreds about (mostly American). People still go picnicking and weekend touring! Needless to say the food is marvellous in comparison to England although again some of the things are rationed but there is a never-ending supply of all sorts of fruits… marvellous cakes including angel cakes stuffed with cream! Rather different from Garraways 'stony seedies'!… "

April 22nd 1945 CEW, Office to RCW 552 LCA Flotilla, Naval Party 1768, BFMO Reading

"… We were mighty glad to gather you are in pretty high spirits. But as to the 'Opel' don't bring that home – this is the one I thought of looking into… *{enclosed newspaper clip re GORINGS car captured: … own super-Mercedes… It's the car to end all cars… }*. We watch the Standard every day. It's a bit sensational these days and I'm not sure

---

[96] Operation Anger to retake Arnhem finally was from April 11th -16th 1945 (see Appendix 3)

it's always reliable. The pictures are fearful just now. Are you expecting to see yours there or something?... Grub gets no easier to lay hold of – and looks as though it might get even tighter. M *{OLW}* is still distributing the furniture etc sent by Northampton – twenty van loads I understand - ... M has gone off to Kensington today – some Civil Defence rubbish or other – left me "an egg" for my tea... I do hope you're not taking undue risks out there – careering in jeeps and what not. It sounds a bit like it. Quite enough risks... "

April 29th 1945 (Easter Sunday) CEW to RCW 552 LCA Flotilla, Naval Party 1768, BFMO Reading

"... What news there'll be to report on your next leave which surely can't be so far away!... The papers are rapidly becoming hysterical, contradicting each evening what they print each morning but they're all agreed now we're 'on the way', good and proper... Mrs P and Mary took M to "Arsenic and Old Lace" yesterday afternoon, lunch at the Carlton, tea at the Waldorf – whilst I? – cuppercorfee at Lyons! (Still on the whole, I think I'd prefer it, in all the circs.)... "

May 2nd 1945 RCW, 552 LCA Flotilla, Naval Party 1768, BFMO Reading (censor) to Home

"Here I am again safe and well!... I had seen an almost similar article re Goering's car... in fact I've seen quite a number of really beautiful cars taken from 'Jerry', they did themselves pretty well. I have received an air letter from John in Sydney!... hundreds of cars – stacks of food... unlike the absolute hole I'm living in at the moment – might just as well have joined the army!... I wonder if Hitler is really dead or the whole story is a fake! To get him hidden away somewhere. You simply can't trust any of the 'em... No idea when I shall be getting leave – not before it's finished I think... "

May 6th 1945 (Easter Sunday) CEW, Home to RCW, 552 LCA Flotilla, Naval Party 1768, BFMO Reading

"... I think people here have been strung up so much with V. Day stuff and promises that it will come eventually as an anti-climax – but I can't see much real cause for going mad while there is the Eastern trouble to be settled... Ill news telephoned from B yesterday. TA... *{family & school friend, see letter Nov 1st 1941}* killed – apparently as long ago as February. Instructor pilot he was, came down in North Sea and couldn't be reached before he drowned. Bad, bad... me to write to Mrs A... which I have done as she had asked him if we knew, not having heard from us... We share your wonderment about Lil' Ole Itler, Goering, Goebbels and co. – very mysterious. And Mr Molotov's story of the Polish Emissaries not so good [97]... "

May 13th 1945 (Sunday) CEW, to RCW, 552 LCA Flotilla, Naval Party 1768, BFMO Reading

"... This has been such an upside down week that it has thrown everything out of gear – me and all. The crowds have been terrific, milling about all over the shop. Beer and cigarettes run out – can you wonder? As I came up here early this morning thousands of folk were trekking to town again – apparently to see the K & Q drive to Church. The waste of time has been frightening. Post, telephone service, staff, just about demoralised – as for the papers and their ads – you might better fish. The odd thing has been 'no music', no bands; even they would have done something for those lost gaping milling crowds. I've heard no bands at all... Mrs A writes nice letter saying she is sure you'd be grieved to hear the news... M treats P, M & J, to seats at Blithe Spirit – finishing at the Savoy Grill!... There won't be a lot left of the £50 token of 'Victory Day' I gave M six days ago, for her 'personal needs'. A mistake. Best forget it. The 'Election' fills the air now – creating uneasiness, knocking markets to bits... best to get it over quick – perhaps Churchill will tell us tonight... "

May 15th 1945 RCW, 552 LCA Flotilla c/o GPO (censor) to JRW, RN Barracks, Sydney, Australia

"... I'm still over in Holland but hope to return any day!! Unfortunately I have not been living in the same way as you apparently are – i.e. I've been in ruined towns, no light, heat or water and bad food!!... I have done a great deal of driving and seen many interesting places & things. Including several drives to Belgium to see Hélène – believe me John this is the one!!!! Am taking steps this

---

[97] The disappearance into Soviet jails of 16 Polish emissaries who in March had ventured from London to Moscow at Stalin's invitation. (http://www.winstonchurchill.org/images/finesthour/Vol.01%20No.135.pdf p26/64)

coming leave to try and get her to England – it shouldn't be so difficult now!... Am due for my promotion to Lieutenant on the 19th of this month so next time you see me – look out!! It's about time 2 ½ years with one stripe is too long I think... "

May 15th 1945 RCW, 552 LCA Flotilla c/o GPO (censor) to Home (censor)

"... Well it's over so please accept that as an excuse for my not having written before. I had a fairly quiet time – although the Dutch people, where I am... went quite mad; as I have gathered they did in London!!... Sorry to hear about A... cannot have lasted very long as it was only about the middle of last year that I met him in H's *{Harrods}* and he'd only just started flying... I'm hoping to be on the way home before very long... Hope the food situation will improve by then as I haven't suffered a surfeit of eating up till now. Managed to hear Churchill's speech the other night, was down in Belgium at the time, thought he sounded very tired. The King did quite well a few days earlier... "

May 18th 1945 RCW, On the Way, Holland to Home

" Hope to be home somewhere around the 26th or 27th Love Dick"

May 20th 1945 CEW, Home to RCW, ?where

"... Anyway I imagine you will be along soon – but the 'food situation' here is not exactly anything to rush home for! In fact I think it's worse than before... I've just been telling John, London seems to be suffering a sort of hang-over – and now another holiday... I suppose when you <u>do</u> come you won't know how you stand about everything. We are getting applications for jobs already and the picture doesn't look very re-assuring but I suppose the Government knows what it's doing. – But what price the 'clearing up' – and what price the arguments all starting and what price the Election?... "

June 4th 1945 Mr & Mrs B, Holland to RCW

"Dear Sir, In great dismay we must tell you that our beloved son M *{see fig 33}* has been killed in a flying accident; the 18th of May at Arbroath in Scotland. As you know we have had four wonderful charming days when he visited us in April after an absence of 3 years;

continually we see him before our eyes in his fine and gallant bearing. He was so kind and gentle, as if he felt that this was the last thing he could be and do for us. You have been a witness to these days and to his departure the 1st of May. That is why you will be a

Fig 33 RCW (right) & MB, near Arnhem: April/May 1945 {See letter of June 4th 1945}

partner in our immeasurable pain. Life has lost its worth for us. We have not yet particulars about his death and his funeral (the 22nd of May). Should you hear something about that, we would be very much obliged if you could tell us. Kind regards to you... "

June 7th 1945 RCW Telegram to Home

"Home Friday evening Dick"

June 11th 1945 DB, HMS *Wren* c/o GPO, London to RCW, Home

"... Well you old so and so how goes it, including the young lady from Bruges or is that out of date!... We are on our way to Leith in the Forth for a period to fit new equipment to deal with these yellow types. I'm hoping to be there about six weeks... I have no desire to quit these shores again. I've had enough already... Cheerio... "

June 19th 1945 London Gazette 'Distinguished Service Cross' (see section 4)

June 26th 1945 CEW, Office to RCW 126 (P) Flotilla HMS *Lizard* Hove Sussex

"I'm very proud of you. God bless you. Dad"

July 7th 1945 Auntie Gertie *{CEW's Sister}*, Harrogate to RCW

"Heartiest congratulations on your promotion and award for gallantry, and sincere thanks for your unselfish share in winning the war for us who wait at home. With love and daily thoughts from Auntie Gertie"

Aug 8th 1945 RCW 552 LCA Flotilla c/o FMO Reading to Home

"1) OFF!!!! – probably tomorrow 2) Please forward letters to above address 3) Will let you have all news later... "

Aug 12th 1945 RCW, 552 LCA Flotilla to Home

"... I'm at present in Rotterdam as expected... calling at Ostend at 5 o'clock last Tuesday evening, needless to say by 6 o'clock I was in Bruges, we sailed the next morning... Nothing is due to start until next week – no doubt you'll read about it though in due course... What price the news? At the time of writing this I have heard nothing definite but I feel there's no doubt practically - although this new bomb affair could finish us all just as quickly - I somehow think we are finding out things we're not supposed to know - sort of end of mankind theory... Rotterdam beautiful, clean... open spaces where the 1940 bombing took place... what cars there are seem far more modern than anything I've seen in London... one drawback... mosquitoes... simply swarms... "

Aug 12th 1945 Hélène Geldof to CEW/OLW?

"V.J.Day. *{officially Aug 15th}* My best wishes for this great occasion!!! Hélène Geldof, Bruges"

Aug 17th 1945 RCW, 552 LCA Flotilla c/o FMO Reading to Home

"Over at last!! Seems almost impossible to believe – I don't think I need worry over the Far East now and John stands a good chance of a quicker home-coming at any rate! From D's letters and the newspapers I gather London went quite mad! Even before the surrender was officially announced. It was much more peaceful here although everybody seems much more cheerful – you may have read in the papers that the Naval Exhibition *{Navy Week in Rotterdam}* was opened by Prince Bernhardt yesterday 16th... The people seem most interested and in the town where there are daily parades by the Marine Band in full dress exhibition drills etc people come in thousands! I hope to get some photos of it... I note the markets have certainly cheered up... "

Aug 26th 1945 RCW, 552 LCA Flotilla c/o FMO Reading as above to Home

"Exhibition has finished! but don't expect to return to England for at least another 10 days... terrible weather... brought about a mass return of mosquitoes!... I shall be really glad to get away; in fact we are all of the same opinion... The demob plan has certainly speeded up as far as the Navy is concerned but even now I can see no chance before the end of next year (I am No 42). By the way did you read about the explosion during the first day of this exhibition... Nasty business – tell you details when I'm next home... I notice American Car Manufacturers have been given permission to build as many civilian cars as they like only no tyres!! Still I've no doubt they'll leave us standing... "

Aug 30th 1945 JRW, Hong Kong Club, HK to Home

"Your observations on the car naturally struck me with great interest but... - a Rolls Royce at 9 miles per gallon, God knows how much tax and a couple of chauffeurs needed to drive or push it. No I can't quite tag on with the idea... we are not sailing [home] until Sept 3rd however I am not coming straight through as I have to change ships at Columbo but still I shall be on the way... approx half way through October... hope Hélène is enjoying her stay... "

Sept 5th 1945 RCW, 552 Flotilla c/o FMO Reading to Home

"... The Flotilla Officer gave me a few days leave so I went down to Kapellen (nr Antwerp) to Hélène's Uncle's place and she came up from Brugge... a very pleasant time, glorious weather, meals in the garden quite different from this dreadful hole Rotterdam. Heaven knows why we are still here – we all expected to be in England by now but transport is supposed to be the trouble... probably early October. But better I suppose to have these men scattered around than all sitting in depots at home doing nothing. I've noticed quite a number of cases in the newspapers recently of disturbances breaking out in camps. It's going to be extremely difficult to maintain any sort of discipline at all. So apart from that we sit here by day, stung to death with mosquitoes whilst trying to sleep at night... I expect D is pleased about the recovery in Japanese shares – there's no doubt the rises in some of those Eastern Securities have been remarkable. Somebody must have made a packet... "

Sept 14th 1945 RCW, 552 LCA Flotilla c/o FMO Reading as above to Home

"... post brought me Ds two letters... thank you!... It is a tremendous pick up! Though because I as well as the rest of us are becoming most depressed over the Government's 'demob' scheme and this holding back of officers – at the present rate means I cannot possibly expect to be out before Xmas 1946!!... I still believe there's going to be a lot of trouble with the rank & file, especially if the press carries on its present agitation of the system... This time last week I wrote that I hoped to be on the way by now but the weather has been too bad for our craft at sea. So we are still here, practically raving lunatics with these mosquitoes. It's worse than being in the tropics. Of course the pools of stagnant water lying in the 1940 ruins are mainly responsible. As for my report on the exhibition – I think that will definitely have to wait until I'm back because I have some very strong views which might not be too advisable to put in a letter, in case its opened... absolute waste of money... "

Oct 21st 1945 RCW 126(P) Flotilla, HMS *Tormentor*, Warsash, Hants to Home

"It rather appears that I shall be here for an indefinite period – they are keeping us together (the flotilla) in case the need arises for a similar exhibition as R'tterdam – very unlikely I think. In the meanwhile it's just the routine work for a depot –'wet-nursing' the men!... D has gone home for this one *{weekend}*... The present release system still puts me somewhere near the Autumn of next year although if I'd been a rating it would have come about June or May even. Still the extra few months have been well worth it I think!"

Nov 10th 1945 RCW, 126(P) Flotilla, HMS *Tormentor*, Warsash to Home

"... No news this end except officers 'demob' is to reach 29 now by the end of Dec: (for Combined Operations only – that's me). It's a big speed up and if they carry on at that rate I may be out by April or early May. In my spare time I have become 'chief of effects' for the play 'The Ghost Train' –starting here on Monday for 3 days!!! Although I say it myself – the train effects we've managed to produce are quite the best part of the play! It's just for the benefits of the troops and some friends of the Captain... Only one Labour gain? That's rather odd isn't it? I expected all the old councillors to be swept right out of the Town Hall... PS D's release is due, middle of next month!"

Nov 17th 1945 RCW, 126(P) Flotilla, HMS *Tormentor*, Warsash to Home

"... D has gone on leave pending demob 10th of next month. My date about 10th April... The Flotilla was disbanded last week – fancy almost 3 years to a day! Now I'm just looking after a great crowd of men with absolutely no interest in life other than release... "

Dec 4th 1945 RCW, 126(P) Flotilla, HMS *Tormentor*, Warsash to Home

"... As for Christmas I should be able to make it from 21st to 27th unless anything unforeseen should happen... The Ghost Train plus 'noises off' goes on tour for 2 evenings to two early RAF stations – quite a run isn't it?... "

1946

Jan 5th 1946 RCW, HMS *Tormentor* Warsash, Hants to JRW, Rose Bay

"... The biggest piece of news from my quarter is that I have made an application for a permanent commission in the R.N.! – now keep your hair on because I really have given the matter a lot of thought and discussed it freely at home. Really the thought of returning to that awful hum-drum of London life is more than I could stand!! Aren't you inclined to agree?... "

Jan 10th 1946 RCW, HMS *Tormentor* Warsash, Hants to JRW as above

"... I do not feel that I shall be here much longer as this place is closing down for keeps very shortly. After this month then I may go anywhere. Did I tell you that I could have been a 'civvy' on Feb 4th! but had to sign on for further service simply because nothing had come through about my application for the R.N. and naturally once I had been released under Class A there wouldn't have been a hope of getting in permanently. In any case... you must see what an unsavoury proposition civilian life is over here at present further cuts expected in food and petrol... Things are worse over here now than in 1941-2 and if one's not a specialist in any line (I'm not!) conditions are worse than ever. On the other hand all the time I'm in the service – I'm able to save pretty steadily. I reckoned that if I were to return to DH's *{DH Evans}* and get say £4 or £5 a week (that's being optimistic) - after travelling to and fro, meals etc it would hardly be possible to save a bob!... PPS No hope of getting Hélène over yet PPSS You've certainly saved us with the food parcels"

Mar 12th 1946 LH *{family friend}*, Robin Hoods Bay, Yorks to RCW, Home

"Dear Dick I have just been released & temporarily... have started work in the office *{Whitby Gazette}*... "

Mar 14th 1946 RCW, HMS *Tormentor*, Warsash to Home

"... I do know that my application has gone to the Secretary of the Admiralty which means that it has gone past the Commodore... which is something. The Captain here gave me a very good 'write up' indeed *{see page 41 bottom}*. (I accidentally saw a copy on his secretary's desk) so there's nothing more I can do here but hope for the best! As regards my feelings about it I can only say that I've been very happy in the service during wartime and I think I can say I've made a reasonable showing at it; so I feel that in peace-time there's no reason at all to suppose once started off, I shouldn't do just as well. Apart from that it does provide a certain amount or even a great deal of the outdoor existence which of course you know has a great attraction for me as well as being – in my case anyway – a physical benefit. I'm more than certain that I shouldn't be happy confined to an office and naturally that being the case couldn't possibly make a 'go' of it… secure… a certain 'status'… perfectly happy in my decision… "

Apr 3rd 1946 RCW, Lowestoft, Suffolk to Home

"Address: HMS *Mylodon* GPO Box 200, Lowestoft, Suffolk. Won't be on board the ship for at least 2 more weeks. Dick."

Apr 8th 1946 CEW, Home to RCW, HMS *Mylodon* (see Fig 4 p20)

"… R called me privately into his room – said he'd seen you and gathered you would be returning to civil life – which I said so far as I know was not quite settled but more than possible. He went on "I'd like to have him here… if he was interested in the work, he'd do well"… so there my boy is a job… without your applying – just offered outright by the Chairman himself… "

Apr 14th 1946 RCW, HMS *Mylodon* HM L.C.I (L) 282 Lowestoft, Suffolk to Home

"… Yes I agree those remarks of R's shouldn't be passed over too lightly – it certainly seems an absolutely first class opportunity… As for the 'budget' – a very luke-warm affair although I notice the screw being put on the "rich" by increasing 'death duties' anyway it seems to have started the stock moving… The ship is now here and we've been working hard on her (cleaning up) all this last week and I should imagine we shall be sailing down to London any time after next weekend… "

Apr 25th 1946 RCW, HMLCI (L) 282 c/o GPO London to OLW, Home

"… Will you write post haste to the Balkan Sobranie Co… asking them to forward to [me]... 500 of their Duty Free Turkish Cigarettes... enclose a cheque for £2-15-0... "

Jul 31st 1946 RCW, White House Wallington (Home) to CEW 79 Station Parade, Harrogate, Yorks

"... Today has been at least financially bright for me... The Navy sent me my first months proper pay for July *{now based at HMS President, London}* £57 with income tax already deducted. They pay me £2-0-11 daily which is a great deal more than I had anticipated... You'd better start enquiries for that Rolls quickly – I'm thinking of buying it myself!!!... "

Aug 3rd 1946 RCW (Home) to Sub Lt JR Wiles HM Tug *Rockmount*, c/o BFMO, Hong Kong

"... I have 10 days leave coming next week so expect I'll be off to Bristol at any rate for a few days. By the way Hélène may be coming any time now – I think she's got everything except the British visa – isn't it amazing we can travel to any country in Europe but hardly anybody may come over here! Nobody would want to though – shortage of absolutely everything, fantastically high prices a pound worth around 4/6 pre-war! You're bound to notice tremendous changes nearly all for the worse I fear... It *{a car}* would be a godsend instead of this everlasting train and buses to get anywhere... Think over the car idea in case D *{CEW}* doesn't rise to the occasion!!... "

Aug 26th 1946 JRW, Hong Kong Club to RCW, Home Wallington

"... I'm in full agreement with your ideas about the car and think negotiations should get under way immediately... I shall be home I expect within the next two months... I'm enjoying my stay in Hong Kong and as you will see I have now left the ship and go under that wonderful denomination "awaiting passage to U.K. for class A release"... "

Dec 27th 1946 B, Holland to RCW, Home

{See previous letter June 4th 1945}

"... very nice not to have forgotten us... I send you and to Miss Hélène my best wishes... A new disaster has overwhelmed me and my daughter. September 18th my dear wife has died... after a little operation... an embolism... In June *{1945}* we could return to our house in Arnhem. As you know there were no windowpanes, no roof; and living there was no pleasure; practically all has stayed so unchanged and unrepaired till we left that house in December 1945... Poland and Holland both have suffered perhaps most of the war, but both have lost the war, in spite of many sacrifices. No trade with the hinterland of ruined Germany. No colonies, almost 10 millions of inhabitants, no fine prospects... The picture of my son with you at his side, is always on my desk. So I will not forget you. Those were the happiest days of my life, but they were short. In June my wife and I were in Scotland to the grave of our son... "

1947

July 12th 1947 RCW and Hélène Geldof married in Wallington. Lt Dobson (see letters Oct 1st 1944 & Nov 1945) was best man. The reception was at home – White House, Holmwood Gdns, Wallington

Fig 34a From left to right: OLW (RCW's mother), RCW, Hélène, CEW (RCW's father) in garden

July 20th 1947 RCW & HMAJ (married July 12th) to Home from Whitby

"... I take it you saw that the King had sent me 2 post war credits and I have also received my priority dockets for furniture, sheets etc... "

Fig 34b Richard and Hélène Wiles at their wedding

Appendices

Appendix 1

Landing Craft: Some information and ops relevant to RCW in Sicily, Normandy & NW Europe

The abbreviated material below, other than the final paragraph, has been selectively extracted and modified from the article on Wikipedia at the link below[98]. The author references can be seen in the original online reference but have been removed from this text for simplicity.

Manning the LCA

In Royal Navy service LCA were normally crewed by hostilities-only ratings, personnel of the Royal Naval Patrol Service, and officers and ratings of the Royal Navy Volunteer Reserve (RNVR). Approximately 43,500 hostilities-only and 5,500 RNVR officers and ratings crewed the various landing craft types in 1944. Of these, the Royal Canadian Navy (RCN) provided 60 officers and 300 ratings, on the condition that they be formed into specifically Canadian companies.

In July 1943 Royal Marines from the Mobile Naval Bases Defence Organization and other shore units were drafted into the pool to crew the expanding numbers of landing craft being gathered in England for the Normandy invasion. By 1944, 500 Royal Marine

[98] Extracts adapted from: http://en.wikipedia.org/wiki/Landing_Craft_Assault (http://creativecommons.org/licenses/by-sa/3.0/)

officers and 12,500 Marines had become landing craft crew. By 1945, personnel priorities had changed once more. Marines of landing craft flotillas were formed into two infantry brigades to address the manpower shortage in ending the war in Germany ...

A junior naval or Royal Marine officer commanded 3 LCA and was carried aboard one of the craft. The officer relayed signals and orders to the other two craft in the group by signal flags in the earlier part of the war, but by 1944 many of the boats had been fitted with two-way radios. On the wave leader's boat the Sternsheetsman was normally employed as the Signalman but flags, Aldis lamps, and loudhailers were sometimes more reliable than 1940s radio equipment. The communications equipment of the troops being ferried could sometimes prove helpful.

LCA crew

The LCA's crew of four ratings included a Sternsheetsman, whose action station was at the stern to assist in lowering and raising the boat at the davits of the LSI *{Landing Ship, Infantry}*, a Bowman-gunner, whose action station was at the front of the boat to open and close the armoured doors, raise and lower the ramp, and operate the one or two Lewis guns in the armoured gun shelter opposite the steering position, a stoker-mechanic responsible for the engine compartment, and a Coxswain who sat in the armoured steering shelter forward on the starboard side. Though in control of the rudders, the coxswain did not have direct control of the engines and gave instructions to the stoker through voicepipe and telegraph. The craft relayed signals and orders to the other two craft in the group by signal flags in the earlier part of the war, but by 1944 many of the boats had been fitted with two-way radios. The sternsheetsman and bowman were to be available to take over from the coxswain or stoker should they be killed or injured. On longer journeys they might relieve them to rest. They also manned any additional machine guns and operated the kedge anchor, if it was required. In mine fields and among anti-invasion obstacles and rocks a seaman would sit on the bow or stern or move about the sides of his boat piloting or preventing it from hitting the obstacles.

Flotilla size

Normally, a flotilla comprised 12 boats at full complement, though this number was not rigid. The flotilla's size could alter to fit operational requirements or the hoisting capacity of a particular Landing Ship, Infantry. An infantry company would be carried in six LCA. Flotillas were normally assigned to one of the Landing Ships, Infantry. These varied in capacity with smaller ones, such as the 3,975+ ton HMCS *Prince David* able to hoist 6 LCA, and larger ones, such as the nearly 16,000 ton HMS Glengyle Landing Ship, Infantry (Large)(LSI(L)) with room for 13 LCA.

The Sicily Landings

Operation Husky, the invasion of Sicily in July 1943 was the first direct assault on the defended territory of an Axis homeland, and the most complex combined operations expedition yet. All together, 94 LCA were employed in six of the seven landing areas. In addition, new craft and vehicles were used on some beaches in preference to LCA. The results of such innovations were mixed. The majority of LCA were to be found in the Eastern Task Force sector landing initial assault units of the Eighth Army in the Gulf of Noto and around Cape Passero. The Western Task Force employed LCA in landing Seventh Army infantry and Rangers near Licata and Gela.

The date for the invasion, Saturday, 10 July, occurred in the second quarter of the moon. This was not an ideal phase of the moon where the Navy was concerned; complete darkness would have been preferred. Although the Landing Ships of the assault forces approached Sicily in a brilliant waxing moon, which would not set until the vessels had stopped in their lowering positions, the LCA made their approach to the coast in darkness. H-Hour was fixed at 02:45, almost two hours before first light.

On the afternoon of D-1 an unexpected north-westerly gale (force 7) blew up and the invasion fleet's small craft were tossed about. On D-Day itself the sea had calmed considerably as the hours passed, but continued churning from the gale. Joss, Dime, Cent, Bark West, and Bark South Areas experienced heavier seas in the wake of the storm. Bark East, Acid South, and Acid North benefited from somewhat calmer water afforded by being on the leeward of Sicily...

Bark West

Still, the sea was not ideal for landing craft. The diary of one RCN LCA bowman states: "At 12:15 a.m., we were lowered away. It was pretty grim, since there was a great wind and the davits themselves were shaking. When we hit the water our LCAs really took a beating... The soldiers were very seasick and for the first time, I thought I would be a victim. Up in the bow, I swallowed more salt water than I thought existed."

However these unfavourable conditions had a beneficial side effect - the enemy relaxed their guard in the belief that a landing in such conditions was not likely and initial resistance proved less than expected. Newer craft were used in the Sicily invasion such as the DUKW amphibious truck; the landing craft infantry (large) (LCI(L)), and, for the first time in numbers, the much larger landing ship tank (LST Mk 2) - an ocean-going vessel being produced in quantity in the United States - with the capacity for up to eighteen medium tanks. None of these supplanted the LCA in its designed role; none of these new types was intended for the initial assault and the LCA was still vital for first wave transportation on contested shores...

Normandy Landings

On D-Day LCA put troops ashore in the Juno, Gold and Sword areas. The LCA also landed the US infantry formations on either flank of Omaha and the Rangers who assaulted Pointe du Hoc. The westernmost landings [were] in Utah area and the pre-dawn landing on Îles Saint-Marcouf.

The LCA ... was confronted with many challenges on D-Day; some presented by the Neptune plan, others by the enemy defences, and others by the weather. The initial seaborne assault on the Normandy coast broke with Allied practice, hithertofore, in that it was made in daylight. The invasion could occur 6 June because the date satisfied certain preliminary requirements. Of particular concern to landing craft, H-Hour was fixed forty minutes after nautical twilight. H-Hour was also fixed for three hours before high water mark. The tide in the English Channel rises from west to east (high water in Utah area occurs approximately 40 minutes before it occurs in the Sword area), and so some difference in H-Hour were planned among the assault areas in order to provide the initial assault landing craft the full advantage of a rising tide. Among the many variable concerns to be considered by the planners was whether to land below, among, or above the line of Element 'C' obstacles. The sea conditions at many places along the coast (6' waves and 2.7-knot (5.0 km/h) currents) were just at the outside operational limit of the LCA. The setting of the Transportation Area 11 miles (18 km) from shore presented an additional complication for LCA operating in the Western Task Force Area in these conditions...

Utah Area 1944

Two little islands off Utah area presented a potential threat to the invasion forces and became the first French territory liberated by seaborne Allied soldiers on D-Day. **At 04:30, four LCA of 552 Flotilla landed detachments of the US 4th and 24th Cavalry Squadrons on the Îles Saint-Marcouf.** *{bold CMW}* From a navigation perspective this operation presented acute challenges; locating two tiny islets in darkness while weaving through unmarked minefields to touch down on rocky landings. These LCA came from SS *Empire Gauntlet*, the Landing Ship whose LCA also delivered the initial wave of the 1st Battalion, 8th Infantry, US 4th Division, the westernmost seaborne landing of D-Day...

Walcheren and the Scheldt estuary

There was one more notable use of LCA in the war in North Western Europe; the fierce fighting around Walcheren Island and the Western Scheldt in the operations designed to open Antwerp (Battle of the Scheldt) (See Map Appendix 2). Though by mid-September 1944, the majority of amphibious assets had been sent to the Mediterranean to participate in Dragoon, the Royal Navy still had 70 LCA in Portsmouth. Because the approaches precluded the use of destroyers to support the assault, the presence of LCS and other support craft was vital in providing covering fire and warding off the attacks of German craft contesting the landings. The low speed of the LCA made the navigation plans and timing of the infantry assault more challenging due to the Scheldt's 4 and 5-knot (9.3 km/h) currents. Still, No.4 Commando got ashore from the bullet-proof LCA with only two or three casualties under heavy fire. The LCA containing the heavier equipment was sunk by an anti-invasion obstacle. Two hours later, the 5th King's Own Scottish Borderers were also landed from LCA at Flushing. During the balance of the operations around Walcheren LCA were used to ferry troops through the river network and the extensive flooded areas...

LC Assault

LCA flotilla 552 was identified as one of a number of Royal Marine LCA flotilla viz 504–510, 521, 524–529, 533, **535–565**, 570–579, 590–594, 597 and 780." [99]

[99] Information from: http://www.royalmarinesmuseum.co.uk/museumresearch/PDFs/Royal%20Marines%20&%20Landing%20Craft.pdf

Appendix 2

a) Map of Northern Front Oct 16th to Nov 10th 1944 [100]

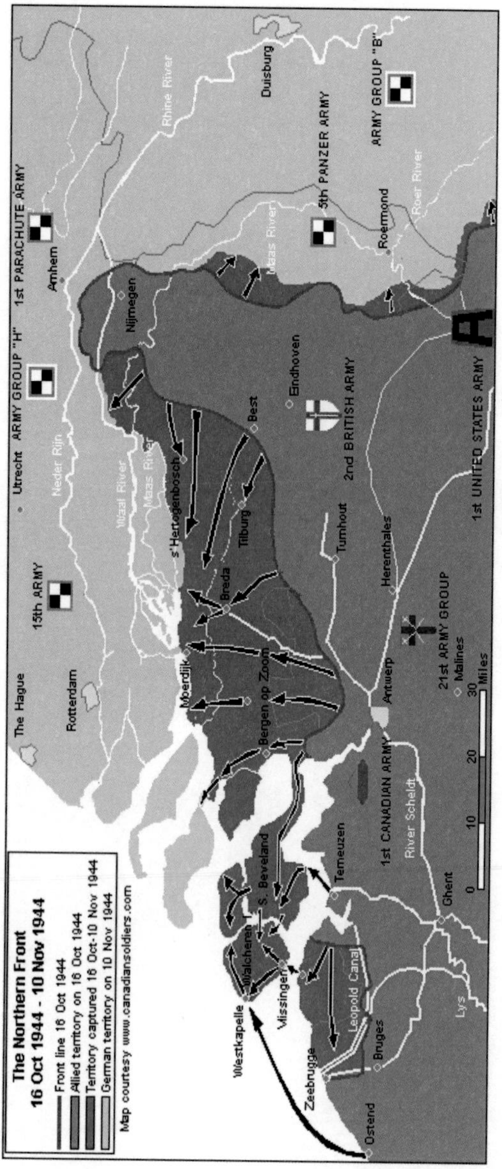

[100] Modified from: http://en.wikipedia.org/wiki/Battle_of_the_Scheldt http://en.wikipedia.org/wiki/File:Mapnorthernfront.gif (map by permission of Michael Dorosh)

b) Map of Allied Ops Lower Rhine Feb to April 1945 [101]

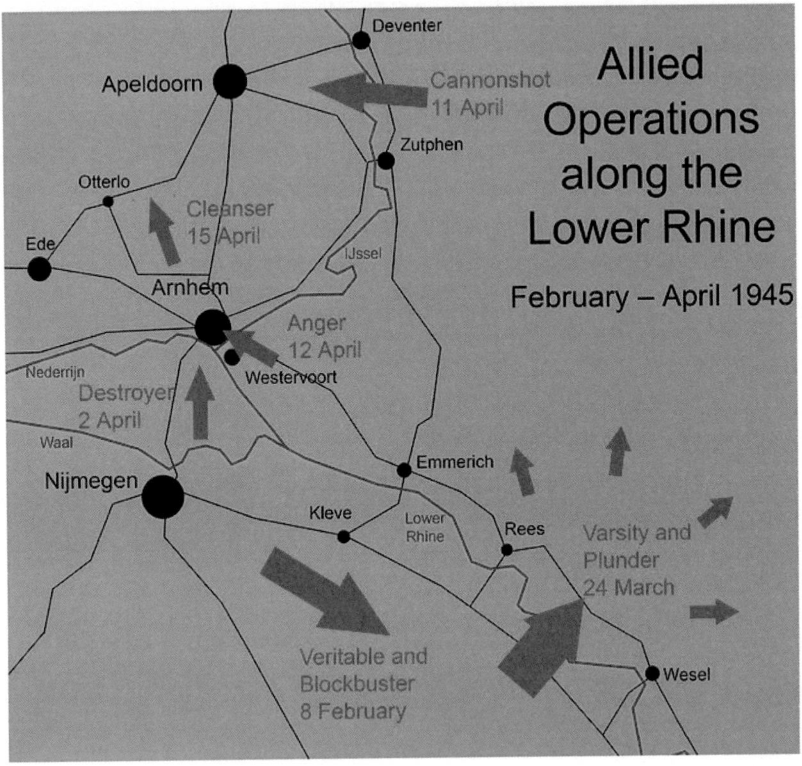

[101] Copied from: Steve Ranger at http://en.wikipedia.org/wiki/File:Arnhem_liberation.jpg (http://creativecommons.org/licenses/by/3.0/deed.en

Appendix 3

a) War diary: Royal Engineers Company 90 March 1945. Reproduced cover & extracts from National Archives WO 171/5452 (with permission).

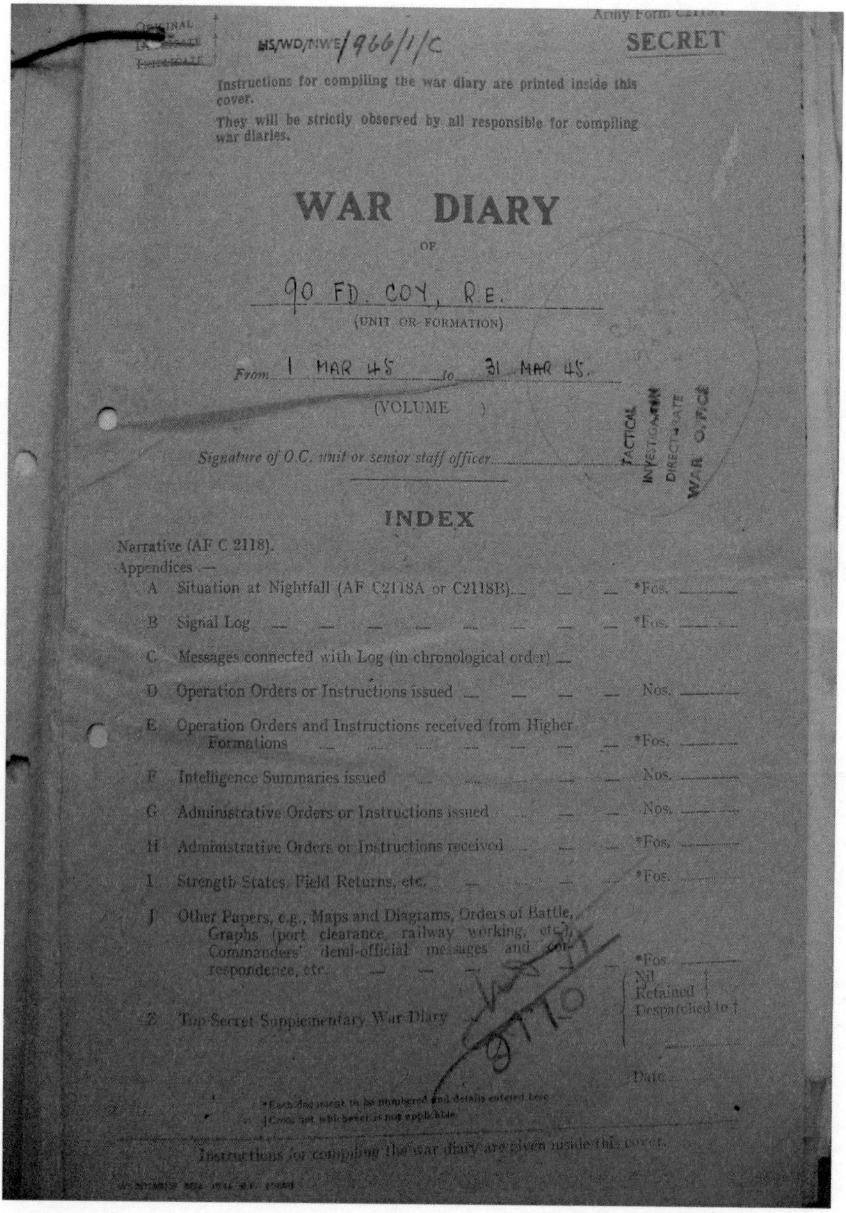

Army Form C2119

HS/WD/NWE/966/1/C

SECRET

Instructions for compiling the war diary are printed inside this cover.

They will be strictly observed by all responsible for compiling war diaries.

WAR DIARY

OF

90 FD. COY, R.E.

(UNIT OR FORMATION)

From 1 MAR 45 to 31 MAR 45.

(VOLUME)

Signature of O.C. unit or senior staff officer

TACTICAL INVESTIGATION DIRECTORATE WAR OFFICE

INDEX

Narrative (AF C 2118).

Appendices —

A	Situation at Nightfall (AF C2118A or C2118B)	*Fos.
B	Signal Log	*Fos.
C	Messages connected with Log (in chronological order)	
D	Operation Orders or Instructions issued	Nos.
E	Operation Orders and Instructions received from Higher Formations	*Fos.
F	Intelligence Summaries issued	Nos.
G	Administrative Orders or Instructions issued	Nos.
H	Administrative Orders or Instructions received	*Fos.
I	Strength States, Field Returns, etc.	*Fos.
J	Other Papers, e.g., Maps and Diagrams, Orders of Battle, Graphs (port clearance, railway working, etc.), Commanders' demi-official messages and correspondence, etc.	*Fos.
Z	Top Secret Supplementary War Diary	Nil / Retained / Despatched to †

Date

*Each document to be numbered and details entered here.

†Cross out whichever is not applicable.

Instructions for compiling the war diary are given inside this cover.

Extracts from RE Co'y 90 diary in National Archive documents WO 171.5452 Royal Engineers Company 90 around the time of 552 LCA flotilla's attachment:

Feb 12th 1945: Report on laying SWR across the Waal: "Object... The requirement was to examine the feasibility of laying 2000ft ½" dia... SWR across 2000 ft of the R Waal in flood using service eqpt."

Feb 15th 1945: "90Fd Coy took over for maint the NIJMEGEN-GRAVE rd from excl the br over the MAAS – WAAL Canal to incl the rd br over the MEUSE at GRAVE... "

Feb 20th 1945: "... const motor boat shed Pwer House Basin; maint approach red to Power House; 3 pl – Maint Tower Br route; constr of Naval wardroom at Power House..." *{see photographs of Powerhouse (sic) and 552 flotilla mess taken by RCW – Figs 14 and 15}*

Feb 27th 1945: "... Nissen Hut (Naval Mess) continued building... "

Mar 1st 1945: "... Building Nissen hut as naval mess. At approx 1630 hrs Spr Sanford WA was killed by Anti-personnel mine on verge of Beek Rd."

Mar 5th 1945: "... Nissen hut handed over to naval personnel"

Mar 9th 1945: "... 552 LCA Flotilla - Dvr – wholetime – 552 LCA Flotilla possess a 3 ton lorry, but have not dvr"

Mar 23rd-26th 1945: "Op "Plunder": (1) Preparations & preliminary orders for the crossing of the RHINE are att. (2) 8 GHQ Tps (incl 90 Fd Coy RE) were under comd 13 AGRE for this crossing. 13 AGRE were under comd 30 Corps. (3) 8 GHQ Tps role was to constuct CL 40 BPB at REES. The site selected was the ferry site from 074515 to 074519 (4) From our point of view the following comments on the op may be of interest:-a. The building of the br depended absolutely on the complete clearance of the enemy from REES. Because of this, work could not be started before 1900 hrs 25 Mar. The br could have been started 24 hrs sooner at about MR 038519 b. Instead of this, 90 Coy was put onto building a Cl 40 ferry on this site on 25 Mar. This resulted in the Coy starting the Br tired and undoubtedly added to the time taken. This ferry was handed over to another fmn for op & was only used for a few loads, after which it drifted downstream &

destroyed a Cl 9 FBE br & fouled a 50/60 raft... (5) Lessons, then, are:- (a) Flexibility in planning as to final selection of site which must depend on the tactical development of the assault crossing. (b) Tps *{troops}* earmarked for CL 40 br must not be sidetracked on to odd jobs, but must be kept fresh. (c) While technical details, including possible alternatives, must of course be planned out beforehand, flexibility must be retained."

b) Ops relating to Liberation of Arnhem 1945. The abbreviated and selected extracts below have been modified from article[102]. The author references can be seen in the original online reference but have been removed from this text for simplicity.

Extract 1

Operation Anger (sometimes known as **Operation Quick Anger**), was a military operation to seize the city of Arnhem in April 1945, during the closing stages of the Second World War. It is occasionally referred to as the **Second Battle of Arnhem** or the **Liberation of Arnhem**. The operation was part of the Canadian First Army's liberation of the Netherlands and was led by the British 49th (West Riding) Division, supported by armour of the 5th Canadian (Armoured) Division, Royal Air Force air strikes and boats of the Royal Navy.

Extract 2

Allied Crossing of the Lower Rhine

In February 1945 the Allies launched Operations Veritable and Grenade, striking east from land captured during Market Garden directly into Germany. These paved the way for Operations Plunder and Varsity, crossing the River Rhine further upstream from Arnhem. 21st Army Group then advanced rapidly into north-west Germany. Whilst the British 2nd Army advanced west, General Henry Crerar's Canadian First Army was given the task of liberating the Netherlands.

The Canadian Army had been instructed to plan advances across the Lower Rhine when it first assumed responsibility for the Nijmegen salient in November, but any plans were delayed by the winter and

[102] http://en.wikipedia.org/wiki/Liberation_of_Arnhem#cite_note-Whiting159-34
http://creativecommons.org/licenses/by-sa/3.0/

the subsequent allocation of resources for Operation Veritable. However, after Operation Veritable Crerar saw advantages to seizing Arnhem and opening a route to Emmerich during the coming crossing of the Rhine. The first draft of the plan to take the city – known as Operation Anger – was compiled in February as a subsidiary operation to Plunder, but Lieutenant General Charles Foulkes, commander of the recently arrived I Canadian Corps, thought it safer to wait until the Rhine had been crossed before launching an action on Arnhem, and Anger was shelved.

Major Allied operations along the Lower Rhine in **1945**.

... The original (February) plan for Operation Anger had called for an immediate crossing of the Nederrijn near Oosterbeek as soon as the river was reached, if the situation allowed it (Operation Quick Anger)... However, Crerar had ruled that operations could not be made against Arnhem until II Corps had crossed the IJssel and advanced on Apeldoorn, and so Anger could not yet proceed. Additionally reconnaissance patrols on 3 and 4 April determined that German observation posts and positions on the Westerbouwing Heights overlooking the river would make crossing the Nederrijn dangerous. Attempts were made to create smokescreens obscuring the southern bank of the Nederrijn from the watching Germans, a technique that had proved successful in the build up to Operation Plunder. The screen stretched from the town of Randwijk, 10 miles (16 km) west of Arnhem,along the south bank of the river to Huissen, south of Arnhem, but strong winds and a lack of appropriate generators reduced its effectiveness. Additionally the ground on the Island was deteriorating and on 7 April, after considering various alternatives, Foulkes decided Arnhem must be attacked from the east, across the IJssel.

Allied forces

... The attack was planned to proceed in three phases. The initial assault would be carried out by the British 56th Infantry Brigade who would cross the IJssel at night in Buffalo IVs of The Ontario Regiment before clearing the eastern and southern districts of the city. In phase two, the British 146th Infantry Brigade would move forward and attack the high ground north of Arnhem. In the third phase, the

British 147th Infantry Brigade would advance through 56th's positions and secure the high ground and north bank of the Nederrijn west of the city. With the heights around Arnhem secure the 5th Canadian (Armoured) Division would advance through the city and I Corps would resume its advance west. The British took several Canadian units under command along with Churchill Crocodile tanks of the British 79th Armoured Division. Most of the 1st Canadian Infantry Division and 5th Canadian (Armoured) Division were placed in support, and a composite group known as Murphyforce provided a diversion south of the Nederrijn.

The river crossing would be assisted by **552 Landing Craft Flotilla of the Royal Navy who provided several landing craft previously used in Plunder**, *{CMW bold}* and the Royal Army Service Corps (RASC) would run DUKWs across the river during the operation. I Corps' Royal Canadian Engineers (RCE), would build four Bailey pontoon ferries as soon as locations on the enemy bank were captured (two across the IJssel and two across the Nederrijn)...

Phase three The 147th Brigade crossed the Nederrijn from the Island overnight and by the morning of the 14 April they were ready to move through 56th Brigade's positions... By the end of the day the Allied units had reached all of their objectives and most of Arnhem was secure... On the 15 April the Duke of Wellingtons occupied the city's zoo and upon discovering a live polar bear offered it to their brigade commander, who declined. **The Germans were cleared out of the precinct of Velp** *{CMW bold - Velp was where MB and family - fig 33 lived}* and the surrounding area on the 15 and 16 April, bringing Operation Anger to an end.

Aftermath The Allies liberated a ruined city. After the looting the previous year, houses were little more than empty wrecks – devoid of furniture, household goods and even doors. Canadian Broadcasting Corporation correspondent Matthew Halton described the city as "a deserted, burning shell" and the 49th Division war diary noted that "a town had never been more wantonly destroyed." Evidence of the first battle of Arnhem lay everywhere and the liberation was likened to "entering an ancient tomb" ...

Appendix 4

DSC documentation

Copy of front page of file & 2 pages pertaining to RCW (National Archives ADM 1/30302 with permission

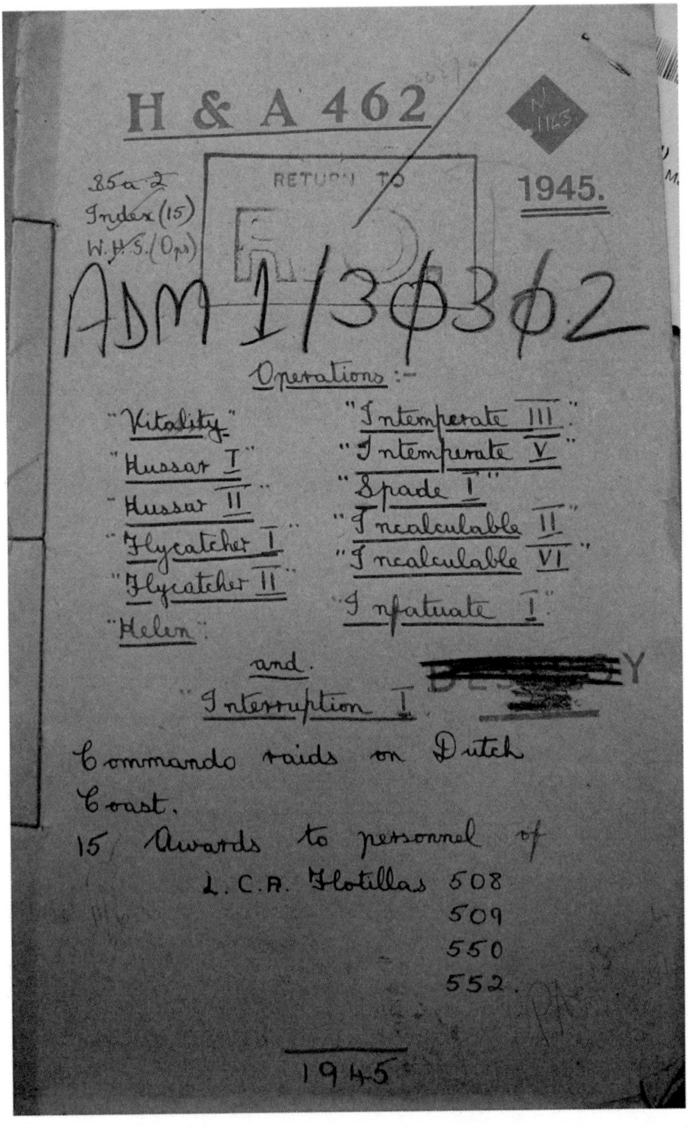

H & A 462

~~85a 2~~
Index (15)
W.H.S.(Ops)

RETURN TO

1945.

ADM 1/30302

Operations:-

"Vitality"
"Hussar I"
"Hussar II"
"Flycatcher I"
"Flycatcher II"
"Helen"
"Intemperate III"
"Intemperate V"
"Spade I"
"Incalculable II"
"Incalculable VI"
"Infatuate I"

and [redacted]

"Interruption I"

Commando raids on Dutch Coast.

15 Awards to personnel of L.C.A. Flotillas 508
509
550
552.

1945

Ship etc. 552 L.C.A. Flotilla Date 26th March 1945

Recommendation for Decoration or Mention in Despatches.

Full Surname WILES

Full Christian Names RICHARD CHARLES

Place of Residence WHITE HOUSE HOLMWOOD GARDENS
WALLINGTON SURREY.

Rank or Rating. (State whether R.N., R.N.R., R.N.V.R., R.N.P.S., R.A.N., ETC.) T. Sub Lieut. RNVR

Official No. —

Port Division —

Whether already decorated (Give particulars and date of publication of award.) —

Whether already Mentioned in Despatches (Give date of publication of award) —

Whether already recommended (Sate date and by whom) YES. 14th March 1945
Flotilla Officer.

Whether previously recommended (If so give particulars) YES.
By 'H' L.C.A. in November (Walcheren)

Whether now recommended for Award of Decoration Decoration

or Mention in Despatches

Whether recommendation is for Immediate, Operational, or Periodic Award. Immediate

Capacity in which employed Divisional Officer

BRIEF DESCRIPTION OF ACTION OR OPERATION.

The landing of a company of the Royal Scots Fusiliers at a point 4 miles up stream from Nijmegen on the North Bank of the river Waal. Map reference 7765 (S.E. of Haalderen)

Specific Act or Service for which
Officer or man is recommended.

Sub. Lieut. Wiles was responsible for the four craft taking p-
in the operation ~~+~~ navigated them to the exact landing
with great skill although for the last ¼ mile the craft were
small arms fire. He remained on the beach for 35 minutes
his craft (L.C.A. 1042) and with the help of a seaman (A.B. Arm-
assisted in evacuating seven casualties. After he had asce-
that there were no further casualties to be evacuated he left
beach which was still under sporadic fire. The craft was
fire until out of range but
casualties were safely evacuated at Nijmegen

Signature of Commanding Officer.

Lt. R.N.V.R.
Flotilla Officer.

Remarks of intermediate authority.
(if applicable)

Strongly recommended.

Lieutenant Commander. R.N.
Squadron Commander.

Remarks and signature of Administrative
Authority.

This operation was remarked upon in para.32 of my Report No. 0600/OP.2 of 3rd April, and was carried out in the most able and courageous manner by 4 L.C.A. under the immediate command of Sub-Lt. Wiles, who is strongly recommended for an award.

(A. F. PUGSLEY)
CAPTAIN, ROYAL NAVY.

Office of Naval Commander, Force "T".
4th April, 1945.

Remarks of Commander-in-Chief.

Concur for Operational award.

ADMIRAL.
ALLIED NAVAL COMMANDER-IN-CHIEF, EXPEDITIONARY FORCE.

Fig 35 The approximate point on the River Waal referred to in the description of the action leading to award of DSC (4 miles upstream from Nijmegen, S.E. of Haalderen) photographed by CMW in May 2011